The Country Show
Cookbook

The
Country Show
Cookbook

Award-winning recipes
from country shows

NEW
HOLLAND

First published in Australia in 2010 by
New Holland Publishers (Australia) Pty Ltd
Sydney • Auckland • London • Cape Town

www.newholland.com.au

1/66 Gibbes Street Chatswood NSW 2067 Australia
218 Lake Road Northcote Auckland New Zealand
86 Edgware Road London W2 2EA United Kingdom
80 McKenzie Street Cape Town 8001 South Africa

The authors and publishers have made every effort to ensure the information in this book was correct at the time of going
to press.

National Library of Australia Cataloguing-in-Publication Data:

Country show cookbook : show winning recipes / compiler,
Agricultural Societies Council.

9781741109764 (hbk.)

Includes index.

Cookery.

Other Authors/Contributors:
        Agricultural Societies Council of N.S.W.

641.5

Commissioning editor: Diane Jardine
Publishing manager: Lliane Clarke
Designer: Amanda Tarlau
Food photographer: Graeme Gillies
Production manager: Olga Dementiev
Printer: Toppan Leefung Printing Limited

Food stylist: Trish Heagerty

Cover: Banana cake, Sue Fischer, Grafton Show, photographer Graeme Gillies

Contents

Acknowledgements

With special thanks to the following members who assisted with the baking for the photoshoot:

Judy Henderson and Judy Skinner, Mendooran PAH&I Association Inc

Lyn Williams and Barbara Crook, Hawkesbury District Agricultural Association

and to

Lyne Fuller, Heather Williams, Castle Hill District Agricultural Society Inc
for their assistance in baking and recipe review.

Introduction

It has been one of the great traditions of country shows to have a cooking section as a major part of their repertoire; a tradition that means so much to country people.

Cooking is something everyone loves and there is so much knowledge and talent amongst our members that we felt a cookbook filled with prize-winning recipes was obvious. We requested all our show societies to send in a selection of their prize-wining recipes. It has been a long and arduous task collecting and compiling all the recipes from all the show societies, but I believe we have a great cross section, not only in geographical terms but in the tremendous variety of prize-winning recipes.

Of course a project of this magnitude could not have taken place if it wasn't for the help of lot of people. First to all those wonderful prize-winning cooks who submitted their recipes. I'd have thought you would have more success extracting the fangs from an irritated tiger snake than a secret recipe from of a show winner, but that wasn't the case— everybody was so agreeable and very forthcoming and we were inundated with nearly 400 recipes. The task of whittling them down was a difficult one and we were sorry that space didn't allow us to publish every single one—every recipe was a winner and we tried to choose a recipe for every show that submitted one.

Secondly to all the women that travelled to Sydney for the cooking and photography session, thank you for your time and effort and a job well done. To all the ASC delegates who chased up recipes and Murray Wilton, and Diane Jardine from New Holland Publishers—without them this book may not have happened.

All the cooks across this wide brown land, you have absolutely no excuse to not win a prize at your next local show, or to not serve up a treat to family and friends, because for the first time we have the ultimate cookbook produced by champions for champions. Sit back relax enjoy the read over a cup of tea and a freshly cooked batch of scones.

David Moor, Warialda
President
Agricultural Societies Council

Scones, pikelets & muffins

Scones

Ruby Mulley, Camden Show

Ruby has been exhibiting at Camden show continually for 50 years and has been the Most Successful Exhibitor on many occasions. This is her basic scone recipe.

Ingredients

3 cups self-raising flour
4 teaspoons icing sugar
1½ level teaspoons baking powder
1 level teaspoon salt
large ½ cup thickened cream
$^2/_3$ cup milk
½ cup hot water

Method

Preheat oven to 230°C (450°F).
Sift all dry ingredients into a bowl 6 times to aereate the ingredients. Make a well in centre and add the cream, milk and water.
Mix with a knife. The ingredients should come together easily without too much effort. If the mixture is too stiff add more milk but don't overwork or the scones will be tough. Turn dough onto a floured board and knead well. Cut with a sharp cutter and place onto slightly greased tray.
Place in oven for 10 minutes.

Makes 10–12

Tip

Mix the dough until it is just combined— don't overwork it —or the scones will be tough and heavy.

Scones

. . . .

Easy scones

Clive Taylor, Baradine Show

A quick and easy scone recipe.

Ingredients

3 cups self-raising flour
1 cup cream
1 cup lemonade

Method

Preheat oven to 220°C (425°F).
Sift flour into bowl. Make a well in the middle
and add cream and lemonade. Stir with a
table knife until ingredients come together
as a dough. Flour a board and knead dough
lightly. Press into rounds. Place on a greased
tray and cook in oven for 15 minutes.
When cooked, brush top lightly with butter
or margarine.

Makes 6–8

· ·

Pumpkin scones

Elva Jones, Kyogle Show

Elva has been cooking for 60 years. Her cousins were
all great cooks so she just followed the trend.

Ingredients

125g butter
½ cup sugar
1 cup mashed pumpkin, warm
1 teaspoon natural vanilla
1 egg
3 cups self-raising flour
½–¾ cup warm milk
pinch salt

Method

Preheat oven to 230°C (450°F).
Cream butter and sugar together.
Add pumpkin, vanilla and egg.
Then add the flour and milk and mix well.
Turn out onto a floured board and cut with
round cutters.
Cook in oven for 15–20 minutes. When
cooked, wrap in a tea towel to cool.
Note: Different types of pumpkin will alter
the colour and texture of the scones. Jap
pumpkin will require less milk while a dry
pumpkin, such as Queensland Blue, will need
more milk.

Makes 14–16

· ·

Date scones

Margaret Mears, Bulahdelah Show

Ingredients

2 tablespoons cream
2 tablespoons castor sugar
1 cup milk, plus extra for brushing
3 cups self-raising flour
¼ teaspoon salt
1 cup dates, chopped

Method

Preheat oven to 200ºC (400ºF).
Grease and flour a baking tray.
In an electric mixer beat cream and sugar.
Slowly add milk.
Sift the flour and salt together twice and stir
into the creamed mixture. Add the dates and
mix well.
Roll out the dough and cut into round shapes.
Brush with a little milk and bake in oven for
10–12 minutes. Remove from oven and wrap
in a clean towel to cool.

Makes 8–10

Sweet sultana scones

Diane McElwaine, Culcairn Show

As I was taught how to make scones in my younger days, I have taken seniors' licence and amended the 'rub butter into the flour with the tips of the fingers'. My way still makes delicious and award-winning scones.

Ingredients

4 cups of self-raising flour
1 teaspoon cooking salt
125g (4 oz) butter or margarine
½ cup sugar (raw or white), plus extra for top
¾ cup sultanas
1¼ cups milk

Method

Preheat oven to 200ºC (400ºF).
Sift flour and salt together. Melt butter, pour into flour mixture and mix in until it resembles the texture of breadcrumbs. Add sugar and combine.
Add sultanas and milk so that it makes a stiff dough.
Turn out onto a floured surface and level out to about 4cm (1.5 in) thick. Cut with scone cutter and place on baking tray.
Baste with milk and sprinkle sugar on top and bake on middle shelf in oven for 15–20 minutes.

Makes 8–10

Basic pikelets

Bronwyn Partridge, Armidale and New England Show

Ingredients

1 cup of self-raising flour
¼ cup of castor sugar
pinch of bicarbonate soda
1 egg
¾ cup milk

Method

Place all ingredients in a large bowl and beat until creamy.
Heat a non-stick or greased frypan on the stove. Drop dessertspoons of mixture into the pan, allowing sufficient room for pikelets to expand. When bubbles appear, turn carefully with a spatula.
Cook until lightly browned.
Serve with strawberry jam and cream.

Makes 18–20

. . . .

Breakfast savoury pikelets

Christopher Pearson, Armidale and New England Show

Ingredients

3 eggs
pinch of curry powder (optional)
2 slices ham, finely sliced (optional)
1 cup of self-raising flour
¼ cup of castor sugar
¾ cup of full cream milk

Method

Hard-boil 2 of the eggs. Cut eggs into fine slices and add curry powder, if desired.
Place all ingredients in a bowl and beat until creamy. Add the boiled egg and ham, ensuring the mixture is well blended and creamy.
Heat a non-stick or greased frypan on the stove. Drop dessertspoons of mixture into the frying pan, allowing sufficient room for pikelets to expand. When bubbles appear, turn carefully with a spatula. Cook until lightly browned. Can be garnished with shallots or barbeque sauce, as per your taste but definitely no jam or cream!

Makes 18–20

. . . .

Orange poppy seed muffins

Una Greco, Picton Show

Ingredients

2½ cups self-raising flour
¼ cup poppy seeds
⅓ cup castor sugar
125g (4 oz) butter, chopped
⅔ cup orange marmalade
1 cup milk
2 eggs
1 tablespoon grated orange rind
⅓ cup orange marmalade, extra

Method

Preheat the oven to moderately hot 200°C (400°F) or 160°C (325°F) for a fan forced oven. Lightly brush twelve ½-cup muffin holes with oil or melted butter.

Sift the flour into a bowl. Stir in the poppy seeds and sugar and make a well in the centre. Place the butter and marmalade in a small saucepan and stir over low heat until they have combined. Alternatively this can be done in the microwave oven. Cool slightly. Whisk together the milk, eggs and rind in a jug and pour into the well in the flour mixture. Add the butter and marmalade mixture. Fold gently with a metal spoon until just combined. Do not over-mix; the batter should be lumpy. Fill each muffin hole three-quarters full with the mixture. Bake for 20–25 minutes, or until the muffins are risen, golden and come away from the side of the tin.

Heat the extra marmalade and push it through a sieve. Brush generously over the tops of the warm muffins. Allow to cool in the tin for a couple of minutes, then gently loosen each muffin with a flat-bladed knife and lift out onto a tea towel.

Serve at room temperature.

Makes 12

Orange
poppy seed muffins

. . . .

Spicy pumpkin muffins

Jessie Druce, Ardlethan Show

Ingredients

1½ cups self-raising flour
¼ teaspoon nutmeg
¼ teaspoon mixed spice
½ teaspoon salt
½ cup brown sugar
½ cup sultanas
1 egg
¼ cup vegetable oil
½ cup pumpkin, cooked, drained and mashed
½ cup milk

Method

Preheat oven to 180°C (350°F). Grease well a muffin or deep patty tin.
Sift flour, nutmeg, mixed spice and salt in a bowl.
Stir in sugar and sultanas. Beat egg, add oil, pumpkin and milk. Blend thoroughly. Add to dry ingredients and stir until mixed. Turn into muffin tin and bake for 18–20 minutes.

Makes 12

. . . .

Handmade bread

Judy Michell, Narrabri Show

Judy was the first female President of the Narrabri Show Society from 1997 to 2005.

Ingredients

1kg (2.2 lb) plain flour (if using wholemeal flour, use 900g/2 lb)
3 cups warm water (slightly less)
1 tablespoon sugar
28g (1 oz) compressed yeast
1¼ tablespoons salt
1 cup powdered milk
3 tablespoons oil

Method

Preheat oven to 200°C (400°F).
Put 1 cup of the flour, 1 cup warm water, 1 tablespoon sugar and yeast into a bowl and mix. Place in a warm place until light and frothy—about 10–15 minutes.
Place remaining flour and powdered milk in a big bowl. Add yeast mixture, rest of water with the oil and salt mixed in it.
Knead for 5 minutes.
Put dough in a well-greased bowl and place in a warm place until it doubles in bulk.
Punch down and knead well. Place in a bread tin (a proper bread tin gives best results), let it rise to near top of tin.
Place in oven and cook for 30–40 minutes (if using wholemeal cook for 1 hour).

Photo courtesy Rural Press

· ·

Pastry

Phil Fisher, Kiama Show

A sweet pastry recipe that can be used as a base for many other recipes.

Ingredients

115g (3¾ oz) butter
3 tablespoons sugar
1½ cups self-raising flour
1 egg
3 tablespoons custard powder

Method

Cream butter and sugar together.
Add the flour, egg and custard powder and
mix well together.

Cakes

· ·

Cherry cake

Val Hawker, Barellan Show

Ingredients

170g (6 oz) butter or margarine
¾ cup castor sugar
1 teaspoon vanilla
2 eggs, lightly beaten
200g (7 oz) glacé cherries, washed
and chopped in half
1 cup plain flour (reserve 2 tablespoons for
cherries)
1 cup self-raising flour
pinch of salt
⅓ cup of milk

Method

Preheat oven to 170°C (330°F). Grease a
20cm (8 in) cake tin.
Wash cherries in cold water then in hot water
and drain well—cherries must be dry.
Sprinkle 2 tablespoons of flour over cherries
and toss until well coated.
Cream butter or margarine until soft and
creamy. Gradually add sugar and vanilla, then
the eggs. Sift the flours and salt together.
Slowly add the remaining flour to creamed
mixture, alternating with milk.
Lastly add the cherries and fold in.
Pour into tin and bake for approximately
1 hour. Let cool in tin, turn out onto a cake
rack and ice.

Icing

Ingredients

2 cups icing sugar
2 tablespoons butter, soft
juice of 1 lemon

Method

Combine sugar and butter in a bowl and
blend. Add lemon juice to blend and cream
thoroughly until smooth.

Cherry cake

Apple cake

· ·

Apple cake

Nellie McIntyre, Tumbarumba Show

Ingredients

90g (3 oz) margarine
90g (3 oz) sugar plus extra to cook apples
2 eggs
1 tablespoon milk
2 cups self-raising flour
2–3 apples, peeled, cored and sliced

Method

Preheat oven to 180°C (350°F). Grease and line an 18cm (7 in) sponge tin.
Cream margarine and sugar. Add eggs and milk and mix then add flour. Knead the mixture, divide into 2, and roll out. Place one sheet in the bottom of the tin.
Wash the apple slices and place in a small saucepan with a small amount of sugar to taste.There should be enough water on the apple slices to cook until tender. If not, add 1 tablespoon of water.
When the apples are cooked, arrange the hot apples evenly around the tin and cover with the second sheet.
Cook for approximately 20 minutes.

Tip

Roll the pastry between 2 sheets of glad wrap and turn out while hot.

Photo courtesy Rural Press

. . . .

Chocolate butter cake

Nikki Harmer, Cooma Show

This recipe won Nikki the Under 16 Chocolate Cake first prize.

Ingredients

185g (6 oz) butter, chopped
¾ cup castor sugar
3 eggs
1 cup self-raising flour
½ cup plain flour
¹/₃ cup cocoa
½ cup milk

Method

Preheat oven to 180ºC (350ºF).
Grease a deep 20cm (8 in) round cake tin and cover base with baking paper.
Add all ingredients to medium bowl of electric mixer, beat on low speed until ingredients are combined. Then, beat on medium speed until mixture is smooth and changed in colour.
Pour mixture into prepared tin.
Bake in oven 1 hour.
Stand few minutes before turning onto wire rack to cool. Top cold cake with chocolate fudge frosting.

Chocolate fudge frosting

Ingredients

45g (1½ oz) unsalted butter
2 tablespoons water
¼ cup castor sugar
¾ cup icing sugar mixture
2 tablespoons cocoa

Method

Combine butter, water and castor sugar in a small saucepan. Stir over heat, without boiling, until sugar is dissolved.
Sift icing sugar and cocoa into small heatproof bowl, gradually stir in hot butter mixture; cover, refrigerate until thick.
Beat with wooden spoon until mixture is smooth and spreadable.

· ·

Chocolate, ginger & fig cake

Margaret Bilbow, Parkes Show

Ingredients

125g (4 oz) unsalted butter, softened
1 cup soft brown sugar, firmly packed
2 eggs, lightly beaten
1½ cups self-raising flour
⅓ cup cocoa powder
¾ cup milk
⅔ cup dried figs, chopped
⅓ cup glacé ginger, chopped

Method

Preheat oven to 180°C (350°F). Grease a 22cm x 12cm (9 in x 5 in) loaf tin and line the base with baking paper.

Beat the butter and sugar together until pale and creamy. Gradually add the eggs, beating well after each addition. Stir in the sifted flour and cocoa alternately with the milk to make a smooth batter.

Fold in the figs and half the ginger. Spoon the mixture into the prepared tin and smooth the surface. Scatter the remaining ginger over the top. Bake 1 hour or until a skewer comes out clean when inserted into the centre of the cake. Leave the cake to cool in the tin for 5 minutes before inverting onto a wire rack.

· ·

Banana cake

Sue Fischer, Grafton Show

Sue says the best results for this recipe are achieved when using fresh ingredients such as a fresh packet of flour and when the milk and eggs are room temperature. We've used Lola Flint, Peak Hill Show's lemon icing recipe here.

Ingredients

125g (4 oz) butter
1 cup sugar
2 eggs, well beaten
1 teaspoon vanilla
2 tablespoons milk,
1 teaspoon bicarbonate soda
3 bananas, mashed
1½ cups self-raising flour
lemon icing (optional)

Method

Preheat oven to 180°C (350°F). Grease a deep 20cm (8 in) round tin.
Cream butter and sugar until fluffy. Add eggs and combine. Mix through vanilla and milk in which soda has been dissolved.
Add bananas. Fold through flour mixing to an even consistency.
Pour into tin and bake in oven for 35–40 minutes.

Lemon icing

Ingredients

1 dessertspoon butter, soft
1½ cups icing sugar
lemon juice

Method

Combine butter and icing sugar in a bowl. Add enough lemon juice to make a soft paste and mix well.

Banana cake

. . . .

Banana ginger cake

Lola Flint, Peak Hill Show

Ingredients

125g (4 oz) butter
180g (6 oz) sugar
2 eggs
1 tablespoon golden syrup
3 small bananas, mashed
1 cup self-raising flour
1 cup plain flour
½ level teaspoon bicarbonate soda
1 level dessertspoon cinnamon
1½ level dessertspoons ground ginger
½ level teaspoon ground cloves
½ cup milk

Method

Preheat oven to 180°C (350°F). Grease a 28cm x 18cm x 3.8cm (11 in x 7 in x 1½ in) tin. Cream butter and sugar. Add eggs one at a time, then add golden syrup and banana. Sift dry ingredients and add alternately with milk. Pour into tin and bake in oven for 30–35 minutes. When cold spread with lemon icing.

Lemon icing

Ingredients

1 dessertspoon butter, soft
1½ cups icing sugar
lemon juice

Method

Combine butter and icing sugar in a bowl. Add enough lemon juice to make a soft paste and mix well.

Photo courtesy Rural Press

. . . .

Carrot cake

Heather Henry, Camden Show

At 80 years old in 2009, Heather has been exhibiting her cakes for 20 years and was recently awarded a plaque in recognition and appreciation of her long-standing contribution to the Camden Show.

Ingredients

1 cup self-raising flour
1 teaspoon bicarbonate soda
1 teaspoon ground cinnamon
1 cup brown sugar, firmly packed
1½ cups grated carrot
½ cup sultanas
½ cup chopped glacé ginger
½ cup chopped walnuts
2 eggs, lightly beaten
⅔ cup sunflower oil

Method

Preheat oven to 160°C (325°F).
Grease a 15cm x 25cm (6 in x 10 in) loaf tin, line the base with paper and grease the paper. Sift flour, bicarbonate soda and cinnamon into the medium bowl of an electric mixer. Stir in sugar, carrot, sultanas, ginger and walnuts. Combine the eggs and oil and add to flour mixture.
Beat on medium speed for 5 minutes.
Pour mixture into prepared loaf tin and bake for about 55 minutes.
Turn onto wire rack to cool.

Cream cheese icing

Ingredients

115g (4 oz) cream cheese
28g (1 oz) butter
225g (8 oz) icing sugar
1 teaspoon vanilla
walnuts, to decorate

Method

In a small bowl beat together all the ingredients. When the cake is cold, spread with icing.
Decorate with walnut pieces, if desired.

Note: This cake can be frozen for up to 2 months. This recipe is unsuitable to microwave.

Carrot cake

Chocolate cake

Jan Gibson, Cumnock Show

Ingredients

125g (4 oz) butter
1 cup castor sugar
2 eggs
1 cup self-raising flour
2 level tablespoons cocoa
½ cup milk
½ teaspoon of vanilla

Method

Preheat oven to 180°C (350°F). Grease and line a 20cm (8 in) square tin.
Cream butter and castor sugar until light and creamy. Add the eggs, one at a time, mixing well. Sift flour and cocoa together and then add to mixture, alternately with the milk and vanilla combined. Don't overmix. Pour into tin and bake in oven for 30–35 minutes.

Tip

When making chocolate cakes add some cocoa to the flour when dusting the pan to prevent white streaks on the crust.

Chocolate beetroot cake

Joyce Brisbin, Mullumbimby Show

Ingredients

1 cup vegetable oil
1¼ cups castor sugar
1 teaspoon vanilla
1 cup cooked and pureed beetroot
3 eggs, beaten
1½ cups self-raising flour
½ cup cocoa

Method

Preheat oven to 150°C (300°F) for fan-forced oven or 170°C (330°F) for conventional oven. Grease a 20cm (8 in) cake tin.
Mix together oil, sugar, vanilla and beetroot. Gradually add eggs. Stir in sifted flour and cocoa.
Pour into tin and bake in oven for 70 minutes.

· ·

Moist and easy chocolate cake

Barbara Potter, Morisset/Lake Macquarie Show

Ingredients

1½ cups plain flour
1 teaspoon bicarbonate soda
½ teaspoon salt
3 tablespoons cocoa
1 cup sugar
3 tablespoons oil
1 tablespoon vinegar
1 teaspoon vanilla

Method

Preheat oven to 250°C (485°F). Grease a
29cm (12 in) round tin
Sift and combine in a bowl plain flour,
bicarbonate soda, salt, cocoa and sugar.
Make three holes in the dry mixture, into hole
1 put the oil, into hole 2 put the vinegar and
into hole 3 put the vanilla. Pour 1 cup of cold
water over the mixture and stir with a wooden
spoon until mixture is combined. Pour 1 cup
cold water over all the mixture and stir with
wooden spoon until mixture is combined.
Pour mixture into tin and bake in oven for
20–25 minutes.

Rich chocolate cake

Ellice Schrader, Newcastle Regional Show

Ingredients

185g (6 oz) butter
2 teaspoons vanilla essence
1¾ cups castor sugar
3 eggs
2 cups self-raising flour
²/₃ cup cocoa
1 cup water

Method

Preheat oven to 180° (350°F). Grease a deep 23cm (9 in) round cake tin and line base with greased paper. Combine butter, vanilla, sugar, eggs, sifted flour and cocoa and water in large bowl. Beat on low speed by electric mixer until ingredients are combined. Increase speed to medium, beat about 3 minutes until mix is smooth and changes colour. Spread in prepared tin. Bake for about 90 minutes. Stand 5 minutes before turning out onto wire rack to cool.
Spread cold cake with icing.

Icing

Ingredients

90g (3 oz) margarine
½ cup cocoa
1½ cups icing sugar
2 tablespoons milk

Method

Melt the margarine. When slightly cool add cocoa, icing sugar and milk and mix well. Spread on cake.

Chocolate mud

. . . .

Chocolate mud cake

Leanne Tett, Cobargo Show

Ingredients

250g (8 oz) butter, melted
1 tablespoon coffee powder
1½ cups hot water
200g (7 oz) chopped cooking chocolate
1½ cups castor sugar
1½ cups self-raising flour
¼ cup cocoa
2 eggs
2 teaspoons vanilla

Method

Preheat oven to 150°C (300°F).
Grease and line a 20cm (8 in) tin.
Combine the coffee powder and hot water.
Stir this coffee mixture into the melted butter
with the chocolate and sugar until smooth.
Gradually beat in sifted dry ingredients in
3 lots. Add eggs and vanilla and beat well.
Pour into tin and bake in oven for 1½ hours.
It is important to stand to become completely
cold before turning out. Ice when cold.

Icing

Ingredients

125g (4 oz) unsalted butter
125g (4 oz) cooking chocolate

Method

Melt butter and chocolate together, stirring.
Cool until spreadable.

· ·

Chocolate mug cake

Annette Graham, Coffs Harbour Show

An extremely simple and delicious chocolate cake you can make in one dish
in 5 minutes.

Ingredients

4 tablespoons self-raising flour
4 tablespoons of sugar
2 tablespoons of cocoa
1 egg
3 tablespoons of milk
3 tablespoons of olive oil
1 tablespoon of chocolate chips
dash of vanilla essence
1 large coffee mug

Method

Add all dry ingredients to mug, then add whole egg and mix thoroughly.
Add milk and olive oil and mix thoroughly.
Add chocolate chips and vanilla essence and mix again.
Place mug in microwave for 3 minutes (based on 1000W microwave). Cake will rise above the mug's rim but this is okay, when cooked tip out of mug onto plate then add cream and enjoy while hot.

. . . .

Chocolate slab cake

May Harris, Nambucca River Show

Ingredients

1 cup cocoa
2 cups hot water
250g (8 oz) butter
2½ cups castor sugar
3 cups self-raising flour
1 teaspoon salt
4 eggs

Method

Preheat oven to 180°C (350°F).
Grease a 30cm (11.5 in) x 25cm (10 in) x 4cm
(1.5 in) square cake tin.
Mix cocoa and hot water and leave for 5
minutes. Cream butter and sugar together.
Add eggs. Sift salt and flour together.
Then add flour and cocoa alternately.
Pour into tin and bake for 1 hour, or until
cooked, but test after 45 minutes.
Let cake cool and ice.

Icing

Ingredients

¼ cup cocoa
1 egg
100g (3½ oz) butter
2 cups icing sugar

Method

Combine ingredients in a bowl and
cream together.

. . . .

Jessie's chocolate cake

Jessica Boxsell, Batlow Show

Ingredients

2¼ cups self-raising flour
²/₃ cup cocoa powder
½ teaspoon bicarbonate soda
1 cup castor sugar
2 eggs
¾ cup milk
½ cup olive oil

Method

Preheat oven to 180°C (350°F).
Grease an 18cm (7 in) tin.
Sift flour, cocoa and bicarbonate soda into a bowl. Add sugar and stir to combine and make a well in the centre.
Combine eggs, milk and oil in a jug. Pour into well in centre of flour mix. Stir to combine.
Spoon mixture into tin, making sure it has a smooth surface.
Bake for 40–45 minutes. Remove from oven and stand cake in tin for 5 minutes. Turn out onto wire rack to cool.

Tip

When you take the cake from the oven, it's a good idea to leave the cake in the tin to cool for five minutes before turning onto a wire rack. Don't leave it any longer or it will sweat.

. . . .

Cornflour sponge sandwich

Shirley Downey, Cumnock Show

Ingredients

1 cup cornflour
½ teaspoon bicarbonate soda
1 teaspoon cream of tartar
4 eggs
½ cup castor sugar
vanilla
pinch salt

Method

Preheat oven to 180°C (350°F).
Grease 2 x 20cm (8 in)
deep-sided sponge tins and dust with flour.
Sift cornflour, bicarbonate soda and cream of
tartar 3 times.
In a large bowl, beat eggs, sugar, salt and
vanilla together for 1 minute. Fold in sifted
ingredients. Divide mixture evenly between
tins. Bake in oven for 15 minutes. Turn out
onto a clean tea towel.
When cold, join together with raspberry jam.

Tip

Sift your flour three times to aerate it and remove any
lumps. This helps create a light sponge. Also make sure
your eggs are at room temperature.

Connie's sponge

Connie Thompson, The Rock Show

Ingredients

4 large eggs
¾ cup plain sugar
1 cup plain flour
1 teaspoon baking powder
1 teaspoon butter
2 tablespoons hot water (not boiling)

Method

Preheat oven to 190°C (375°F). Grease a shallow 18cm (7 in) sponge tin. Beat eggs and sugar until thick. Add sifted flour and baking powder. Fold in carefully with spoon. Lastly add the hot water and butter. Bake in oven for 20 minutes. Sponge is cooked when it leaves the side of the tins.

Tip

To avoid rack lines on the cake, turn it out onto a cooling rack lined with a folded tea towel.

Cinnamon sponge

Wynsome Armstrong, Cootamundra Show
Wynsome says this is her dad's favourite cake. It was always his after the show, but with much more filling!

Ingredients

4 large eggs, room temperature
1 cup of castor sugar less 1 tablespoon
1 cup plain flour
2 teaspoons cocoa
2 teaspoons ground cinnamon
1 heaped teaspoon baking powder
5 tablespoons boiling water
1 teaspoon butter, melted

Method

Preheat oven to 180ºC (350ºF). Grease 2 deep 18cm (7 in) sponge tins. Beat eggs together in small mixmaster bowl until thick. Gradually add sugar, beating until all sugar is dissolved. Triple-sift the dry ingredients, the last time over the egg mixture. Lightly fold in. Quickly stir through wet ingredients. Pour half the mixture into each tin and bake in moderate oven for 20–25 minutes.
Turn out onto a cooling rack lined with a folded tea towel (to avoid rack lines in cake). When cool join together with mock cream. Ice with white glacé icing and sprinkle lightly with cinnamon.

Mock cream

Ingredients

125g butter
4 tablespoons castor sugar
4 tablespoons water
1 teaspoon vanilla

Method

Cream butter and sugar really well until it turns very white. Add water, 1 spoon at a time, mixing well after each addition. Add vanilla and mix in.

Glace icing

Ingredients

100g (4oz) icing sugar, sieved
1 tablespoon water

Method

Mix sieved icing sugar with water in a basin. Beat until smooth, add colour and flavouring as required. The icing consistency needs to be thick enough to coat the back of the spoon. If it's too thin add a little more sieved icing sugar, if it's too thick add a few more drops of water, little by little.

Photo courtesy Rural Press

. . . .

Coffee sponge

Judy Hopkins, Gloucester Show

Ingredients

4 eggs, separated
pinch salt
1 small cup sugar
1 tablespoon coffee essence
1 small cup plain flour
4 teaspoons arrowroot
1 teaspoon baking powder
4 tablespoons milk
1 teaspoon butter

Method

Preheat oven to 180ºC (350ºF).
Grease 2 x 20cm (8 in) cake tins.
Beat eggwhites and salt until soft peaks form. Gradually add sugar and beat well between each addition. Add egg yolks and beat until light and thick. Add coffee essence.
Fold in triple-sifted flour, arrowroot and baking powder.
In a small saucepan or in the microwave, boil milk and butter together.
Fold the butter mixture into the main mixture.
Pour mixture into prepared tins and bake for 20 minutes.

. . . .

Sponge cake

Helen Wright, Kyogle Show

Some more variations on the traditional sponge. The cream filling can be flavoured with sugar, sherry or vanilla.

Ingredients

125g (4 oz) castor sugar
4 eggs, separated
70g (2½ oz) cornflour
1 rounded dessertspoon plain flour
1 teaspoon baking powder
vanilla

Method

Preheat oven to 180°C (350°F).
Grease and paper 2 sponge tins.
Beat eggwhites until white and fluffy.
Slowly add the castor sugar and beat until dissolved. Add egg yolks and just beat in, don't over beat. Add vanilla. Meanwhile, sift dry ingredients 3 times. Add the flours to egg mixture and fold in until all mixed. Pour mixture into tins, an equal amount in each. Smooth out top and drop tins on the table 1 or 2 times. Cook for 20 minutes. Turn out on to cake coolers lined with a tea towel. Cover until cold then fill with cream filling or whipped cream.

Sponge cake

Sponge sandwich

Reta Spencer, Barellan Show

Ingredients

4 large eggs, separated
¾ cup castor sugar
1 cup plain flour
1 level teaspoon baking powder
4 tablespoons milk
1 teaspoon butter

Method

Preheat oven to 180°C (350°F).
Grease 2 x 18cm (7 in) tins lightly, dust
with flour and shake to remove excess. It is
important the tins are the correct size.
Beat eggwhites until they are stiff. Gradually
add sugar and beat constantly until thick and
glossy. Add egg yolks.
Sift flour and baking powder 3 times and
fold gently and evenly into egg mixture.
Boil milk, add butter and quickly fold it into
the mixture. Pour into tins evenly and bake
for approximately 20 minutes. Sponge will
spring back when lightly touched with fingers.

· ·

Fielders sponge

Jean Wills, Trundle Show

Ingredients

4 eggs, separated
¾ cup castor sugar
¾ cup cornflour
1 teaspoon baking powder
1 teaspoon cream of tartar
1 teaspoon vanilla
pinch salt
cream, to serve
strawberries, to serve

Method

Preheat oven to 180°C (350°F).
Grease 2 x 20cm (8 in) sponge tins.
Sift dry ingredients four or five times. Beat eggwhites until thickened, then add sugar gradually. Add egg yolks, one at a time, alternately with sifted dry ingredients. Add vanilla. Pour evenly into sponge tins. Bake 15–20 minutes; when cake leaves sides of tin remove from oven. If the cake is overcooked it will sink. Fill and top with cream and strawberries.

· ·

Sponge sandwich

Faye Wheeler, Dubbo Show

Ingredients

4 large (65g) eggs, farm fresh and room
temperature
170g (6 oz) castor sugar
165g (5¼ oz) self-raising flour
pinch of salt
4 tablespoons hot water
20g (²/₃ oz) butter
1 teaspoon vanilla
jam, to serve
whipped cream, to serve
icing sugar, to serve

Method

Preheat oven to 180ºC (350ºF). Grease and lightly flour two deep 18cm (7 in) sandwich tins—it also helps to line with baking paper first. Beat eggs well until they are thick and creamy. Add sugar gradually, a dessertspoon at a time, beating well after each addition, and add the vanilla. Beat for 5–7 minutes after last sugar is added. Sift flour and salt and fold into egg mixture.

Dissolve butter in hot water, fold into mixture by gently drawing spoon through mixture while moving bowl in opposite direction. Repeat until water and butter mixture is mixed in. Divide the mixture evenly into each tin and bake for about 20 minutes in oven. When cooked, turn onto a cake rack to cool.

Plain sponge cake

Mary Yeo, Mendooran Show

This recipe has won Mary first prize for many years at Mendooran Show.

Ingredients

4 eggs, separated
¾ cup castor sugar
1 level cup self-raising flour
½ teaspooon baking powder
3 tablespoons hot milk

Method

Preheat oven to 180°C (350°F).
Line and grease 2 x 20cm (8 in) tins.
Beat eggwhites until stiff. Gradually add castor sugar until sugar is dissolved. Add egg yolks until the mixture becomes creamy. Transfer to a larger bowl.
Sift flour twice. Fold flour into creamy mixture at small intervals. Lastly, add hot milk until the mixture is creamy and smooth, but do not over-beat. Pour into tins, making sure you have same amounts in both tins and bake for 20 minutes.

Coffee caramel cake

Barbara Payne, The Rock Show

Ingredients

125g (4 oz) butter or margarine, chopped
¾ cup firmly packed brown sugar
1 cup self-raising flour
3 teaspoons instant coffee powder
2 teaspoons vanilla essence
2 eggs
¼ cup custard powder
½ cup milk

Method

Preheat oven to 180°C (350°F).
Grease a 21cm (9 in) baba cake tin or a
20cm x 20cm (8 in) x 5cm (2 in) square tin.
Combine all ingredients in the medium
bowl of an electric mixer. Beat on low speed
until ingredients are combined. Then beat
on medium speed until mixture is smooth
and changes in colour. Spread mixture into
prepared tin. Bake for about 40 minutes.
Let stand for a few minutes before turning
onto wire rack to cool. Ice with coffee or
chocolate icing.

Coffee icing

Ingredients

2 cups icing sugar
2 tablespoons butter, soft
2 teaspoons instant coffee

Method

Combine sugar and butter in a bowl and
blend. Add coffee and a teaspoon hot water to
blend. Cream thoroughly until smooth.

Coconut cake

Ellice Schrader, Newcastle Regional Show

Ingredients

250g (8 oz) butter
1½ cups sugar
4 eggs
3 cups self-raising flour
1 cup coconut
pinch salt
2 cups milk

Method

Preheat oven to 150°C (300°F).
Grease a 22cm (9 in) round tin
Cream butter and sugar together, then add eggs, one at a time. Add sifted flour, coconut and salt alternately with milk.
Pour into tin and cook in oven for approximately 40 minutes.

Tip

To test if a cake is done, insert a fine skewer in the centre and remove. If it comes out clean, the cake is cooked. If it has cake mixture on it, the cake needs to cook further.

. . . .

Coconut cake

Kevin Baldwin, Newcastle Regional Show

This is another version of the popular coconut cake.

Ingredients

125g (4 oz) butter
1 cup castor sugar
½ teaspoon coconut essence
2 eggs
½ cup desiccated coconut
1½ cups self-raising flour
300g (10 oz) carton sour cream
⅓ cup milk

Method

Preheat oven to 180° (350°F). Grease a deep 23cm (9 in) round tin and line with greased paper. Cream butter, sugar and coconut essence until light and fluffy. Beat in eggs, one at a time, until combined. Stir in half the coconut and sifted flour with half the sour cream and milk. Then add remaining ingredients and stir until smooth.
Bake for approximately 60 minutes.
Stand 5 minutes before turning out onto a wire rack to cool before icing with coconut icing.

Coconut icing

Ingredients

2 cups icing sugar
1½ cups coconut
2 eggwhites, lightly beaten
pink food colouring, if desired

Method

Combine sifted icing sugar with coconut in a bowl. Add eggwhites and mix well.
Colour pink if desired.

Coconut cake

Date loaf

Trish Crawley, Baradine Show

This recipe makes 2 loaves—one for now and one for later.

Ingredients

250g (8 oz) chopped dates
1 cup sugar
1 cup boiling water
1 tablespoon margarine or butter
2 cups self-raising flour
½ cup coconut
1 egg, beaten

Method

Preheat oven to 180ºC (350ºF).
Grease and line 2 x bar or loaf tins.
In a large bowl combine the dates, sugar,
water and margarine and stir until margarine
has melted. Leave to cool. Add the flour,
coconut and egg and mix well.
Pour evenly into tins and cook for about
an hour.

· ·

Date and walnut loaf

Jean Monaghan, Gulgong Show

Ingredients

1½ cups self-raising flour
½ cup sugar
½ teaspoon bicarbonate soda
½ teaspoon spice or nutmeg
pinch of salt
1½ tablespoons butter
1 cup water
1 cup chopped dates
few chopped walnuts
1 egg

Method

Preheat oven to 180ºC (350ºF).
Grease a loaf tin.
Sift into a bowl self-raising flour, sugar, bicarbonate soda, spice or nutmeg and salt. Melt in saucepan butter, water, dates and walnuts. Bring to boil and allow to boil for 1 minute. Stand aside to partly cool. Pour into dry ingredients and mix well. Lastly add egg and mix in. Pour into tin and bake for approximately 30 minutes.

Date, fruit & nut loaf

Anne Lesker, Lake Cargelligo Show

This prize-winning recipe was given to Anne by her mother, Mrs Ethel Beake.

Ingredients

1 cup of dates, nuts and/or sultanas,
or a mixture of all three.
1 cup of boiling water,
125g (4 oz) butter or margarine
1 teaspoon bicarbonate soda
2 cups plain flour
1 small cup sugar
1 teaspoon baking powder
1 egg

Method

Preheat oven to 180° (350°F).
Grease a loaf tin.
In a bowl, mix together dates and nuts, water,
butter or margarine and bicarbonate soda
and let cool.
Add the plain flour, sugar, baking powder and
bind together with the egg.
Pour into tin and cook for 40–45 minutes.

Date and nut loaf

. . . .

Fruit cake

Margaret McCarten, Lake Cargelligo Show

Margaret says this is a nice moist cake and a good keeping cake. For a rich, dark fruit cake she says to use a dark brown sugar and add a little more fruit. Again, the fruit needs to be soaked overnight so prepare the day before cooking.

Ingredients

2 x 375g (12 oz) packets mixed fruit
250g (8 oz) dates
60g (2 oz) cherries
60g (2 oz) chopped almonds
packet ginger, if desired
5 tablespoons sherry
2 cups plain flour
60g (2 oz) self-raising flour
5 eggs
250g (8 oz) brown sugar
½ teaspoon salt
1 teaspoon mixed spice
250g (8 oz) margarine or butter

Method

Place mixed fruit, dates, cherries, almonds and ginger in a basin. Pour over sherry, mix well and leave overnight.

The next day, preheat oven to 150°C (300°F). Prepare a 23cm (8 in) cake tin, grease and paper well.

Sift plain flour and self-raising flour together well. Place eggs, sugar, salt and spice and half the sifted flours in a mixing bowl and mix well.

Melt margarine or butter and pour over ingredients in the bowl. Add remaining flour and fruit alternately. Pour into cake tin and bake in oven for 2 hours. If not cooked, reduce to 120°C (250°F) for a further ½ hour.

. . . .

1/2lb rich fruit cake

Pat Hoggan, Singleton Show

Start the recipe the day before to soak the fruit overnight. Pat also uses this recipe for her prize-winning steamed pudding and boiled pudding.

Ingredients

250g (8 oz) raisins, quartered
250g (8 oz) sultanas, halved
250g (8 oz) currants, chopped
60g (2 oz) cherries, chopped
60g (2 oz) dates, chopped
¼ cup rum
225g (7 oz) butter
113g (4 oz) brown sugar
113g (4 oz) white sugar
1 teaspoon salt
1 teaspoon lemon essence
1 teaspoon vanilla essence
60g (2 oz) mixed peel, chopped
5 eggs
255g (9 oz) plain flour
55g (2 oz) self-raising flour
½ teaspoon nutmeg
½ teaspoon cinnamon

Method

Place fruit in a large bowl, add rum and let stand overnight.
The next day, preheat oven to 150°C (300°F). Grease and line well a 20cm (8 in) square cake tin or a 23cm (9 in) round tin.
Cream butter, sugars, salt, vanilla and lemon essences, and mixed peel, then add eggs, one at a time. Sift flour and spices. Fold through a little of the quantity of flour into the fruit. Fold flour into butter mixture and lastly fold in fruit. Spoon into tin and on centre shelf of oven for 2½ hours. Turn back oven to 120°C (250°F) and bake for a further 1½ hours, or until done.

Boiled fruit cake

Betty Bird, Wallamba Show

Start this recipe the day before to allow the fruit to soak overnight for extra depth and flavour.

Ingredients

500g (1 lb) raisins, coarsely chopped
250g (8 oz) sultanas
125g (4 oz) red glacé cherries, coarsely chopped
125g (4 oz) currants
60ml (2 fl oz) brandy
125g (4 oz) butter
1 cup water
½ cup dark brown sugar, firmly packed
½ cup castor sugar
½ teaspoon bicarbonate soda
2 eggs, lightly beaten
185g (6 oz) self-raising flour
185g (6 oz) plain flour
whole pecans, to decorate

Method

Combine fruit and brandy in a large bowl. Cover and stand overnight.

The next day, preheat oven to a slow 150°C (300°F). Line the base and sides of a deep 19cm (7.5 in) square cake tin or deep 23cm (9 in) round cake tin with one layer of brown paper and three thicknesses of baking paper. Combine fruit, butter, water, sugars and bicarbonate soda in a large saucepan. Stir over medium heat until the butter is melted and the sugar dissolved. Bring to the boil. Remove from heat and transfer to a large bowl. Cool.

Stir the eggs into the fruit mixture. Add sifted flours and spread evenly into the prepared tin. Decorate top of cake with pecans if desired. Bake for about 3 hours.

When cooked, cover the cake with foil, wrap in a tea towel and leave until cold.

. . . .

Boiled fruit cake

Susan Constable, Mullumbimby Show

This cake can be prepared and baked the same day.

Ingredients

4½ cups mixed fruit
1½ cups chopped dates
125g (4 oz) cherries, halved
125g (4 oz) butter
¾ cup brown sugar, firmly packed
1 teaspoon mixed spice
½ cup water
½ cup sherry (or rum, brandy or orange juice)
2 eggs
2 tablespoons marmalade
1 cup self-raising flour
1 cup plain flour

Method

Preheat oven to a moderately slow 160°C (325°F).
Chop fruit and dates to the size of small sultanas.
Line a 20cm (8 in) cake tin with two thicknesses of greaseproof or brown paper.
Combine chopped fruit and cherries in saucepan with butter, sugar, spice and water. Stir over heat until butter is melted and bring to boil. Boil uncovered 3 minutes. Remove from heat and let become completely cold. Add sherry, eggs and marmalade mix well.
Add sifted flour and mix well.
Spread evenly into prepared tin and bake for about 2 hours. Remove from oven, cover with foil and cool in the tin. Remove foil and tin, leave lining paper intact and wrap in plastic wrap. This will keep refrigerated for up to a month.

· ·

Rich fruit cake

Peter Lloyd-Jones, Upper Hunter Show

Like all good fruit cake recipes, this one needs the fruit to be soaked overnight.

Ingredients

250g (8 oz) sultanas
250g (8 oz) chopped raisins
250g (8 oz) currants
150g (5 oz) mixed peel, finely cut
100g (3 oz) red glacé cherries, quartered
½ cup Bundaberg rum
250g (8 oz) butter
1 teaspoon almond essence
1 teaspoon vanilla essence
grated rind of 2 lemons
250g (8 oz) soft brown sugar
4 extra large eggs
250g (8 oz) plain flour
60g (2 oz) self-raising flour
½ teaspoon ground ginger
¼ teaspoon nutmeg
½ teaspoon mixed spice
¼ teaspoon cloves

Method

Soak fruit overnight in rum.
The next day, preheat oven to 150°C (300°F).
Line a 20cm (8 in) round or square tin.
Cream butter lightly with almond essence,
vanilla essence and lemon rind. Then add
the brown sugar and eggs, one at a time. Sift
flour with spices four times. Add alternately
the fruit and flour to the creamed mixture
until well combined. Pour into cake tin and
bake for 3½–4 hours. Test centre of cake
with a straw. If it comes out sticky, the cake
is not cooked. When cooked, let cool in tin.
Remove from tin after 24 hours.
To store, wrap in greaseproof paper, then foil.

. . . .

Light fruit cake

Morna Wilson, Gloucester Show

Morna says she is happy to share her recipes, in the hope that other people are able to reach the same level of success with it as she has.

Ingredients

250g (8 oz) butter
1 cup sugar (brown and white)
4–5 eggs
1 teaspoon grated lemon rind
1 tablespoon marmalade
2 cups plain flour
½ cup self-raising flour
½ teaspoon mixed spice
750g (1½ lb) mixed fruit
60g (2 oz) each chopped apricots,
cherries, nuts
1 tablespoon wine
1 tablespoon brandy
a little milk

Method

Preheat oven to 175°C (340°F).
Grease a 20cm (8 in) tin and line with paper.
Cream butter and sugar until light and fluffy.
Add eggs, one at a time, beating well.
Add lemon rind and marmalade. Add sifted dry ingredients, then fruits. Fold in well.
Lastly, add wine, brandy and enough milk so that the mixture is stiff enough to hold together when picked up with a spoon.
Pour into tin. Bake in oven for approximately 3 hours, or until cooked. Reduce heat to 165°C (325°F) after 30 minutes, then reduce again to 150°C (300°F) after another 30 mintues.

Boiled pineapple fruitcake

Trish Crawley, Baradine Show

Baradine Show had 110 cake entries and around 45 jam and pickle entries in 2009—a record. We also have a junior cooking section and the local schools regularly submit entries to all sections of the show, particularly the cooking. The show only lasts for a day. By 5pm the pavilions are devoid of displays and entries, but the celebrations continue into the night.

Ingredients

1 cup sugar
1 small 450g can of pineapple
2 cups mixed fruit
1 teaspoon bicarbonate soda
1 teaspoon mixed spice
125g (4 oz) margarine
1 cup plain flour
1 cup self-raising flour
2 eggs, beaten

Method

Preheat oven to 180ºC (350ºF). Grease and line a 20cm (8 in) round tin. Place sugar, pineapple, mixed fruit, bicarbonate soda, mixed spice and margarine in a saucepan. Bring to boil and simmer for 3 minutes. Remove from heat and let cool completely. Stir in flours and eggs. Pour into tin and bake in oven for about an hour.

· ·

Dark fruit cake

Gaile Hart, Peak Hill Show

This recipe was used by Gaile's grandmother and mother, both winning prizes at the Peak Hill Show. She says her first recollection of her grandmother making fruit cake was of her creaming the butter and sugar by hand, judging the oven heat of the fuel stove with her hands and keeping the fire burning very slowly.
This one needs preparing a few days before.

Ingredients

1kg (2 lb) mixed fruit, chopped
4 tablespoons spirit (anything you like such as sweet sherry, brandy, rum or whisky)
250g (8 oz) butter
250g (8 oz) brown sugar
1 tablespoon treacle
5 eggs
few chopped almonds (optional)
315g (10½ oz) plain flour
¼ teaspoon bicarbonate soda
2 teaspoons cinnamon
½ teaspoon nutmeg

Method

Soak fruit in spirit for 1–2 days.
When ready to make, preheat oven to 140°C (290°F).
Prepare an 18cm (7 in) tin by lining the sides and bottom with cardboard from a cereal box as well as two layers of baking paper.
Cream, butter, sugar and treacle well.
Add eggs, one at a time and beat. Add fruit mixture and almonds, if desired, alternately with sifted dry ingredients. Mix well. Spoon into prepared tin, smoothing as you go. Put several layers
of newspaper around outside of tin and place in oven. Sit in oven on several layers of newspaper on a biscuit tray.
Bake in oven for 4–4½ hours. Leave in tin to cool.

Dundee cake

Esme McRae, Armidale and New England Show

Ingredients

2 cups plain flour
salt
180g (6 oz) butter
¾ cup castor sugar
grated rind of 1 lemon
4 eggs
1 dessertspoon plain flour
90g (3 oz) currants
90g (3 oz) sultanas
90g (3 oz) dates
45g (1½ oz) cherries
45g (1½ oz) lemon peel
almonds, for decoration

Method

Preheat oven to 150°C (300°F).
Grease a 18cm (7 in) round tin.
Cream butter, sugar and rind.
Beat in eggs, adding 1 dessertspoon of flour
to prevent curdling.
Sift flour and salt together.
Stir flour and fruit into mixture.
Pour into tin, arrange almonds on top and
bake in oven for 1¼ hours.

Tip

Because fruitcakes have a long baking time, if the cake is browning too fast, place a sheet of foil the top of the cake.

· ·

Fruit & nut Xmas cake

Marj Hockey, Parkes Show

Marj has been exhibiting at the Parkes Show for more than 60 years.
Due to failing eyesight she needs help with some aspects of her cooking,
but she hasn't lost her touch.

Ingredients

250g (8 oz) dessert dates, stoned
125g (4 oz) glacé pineapple, chopped
125g (4 oz) glacé apricots, chopped
125g (4 oz) red glacé cherries, leave whole
125g (4 oz) green glacé cherries, leave whole
125g (4 oz) whole blanched almonds
250g (8 oz) shelled brazil nuts, leave whole
2 eggs
½ cup brown sugar
1 teaspoon vanilla
1 tablespoon rum
90g (3 oz) butter, softened
½ cup plain flour
½ teaspoon baking powder
pinch salt

Method

Preheat oven to 150°C (300°F). Grease
a 20cm (8 in) ring tin and line with
greaseproof paper.
In a large bowl, mix together all the fruit and
nuts (keep ½ cup nuts for garnish).
Beat eggs until light and fluffy. Add sugar,
vanilla, rum and butter and mix. Combine
the flour, sifted, baking powder and salt and
add to the egg and sugar mixture. Turn cake
mixture into tin and place reserved fruit on
top. Bake in oven for
1½ hours. Let cool in tin. Glaze if desired.

Glaze

Ingredients

1 tablespoon gelatine
1 teaspoon sugar
½ cup water

Method

Combine ingredients in a small saucepan
and stir over medium heat until sugar and
gelatine have dissolved.

. . . .

Rich, light fruit cake

Marj Hockey, Parkes Show

Ingredients

1 teaspoon glycerine
1 desertspoon honey
1 desertspoon marmalade
1 teaspoon vanilla essence
½ teaspoon almond essence
2 tablespoons sherry
2 tablespoons brandy
300g (10 oz) plain flour
1 small teaspoon ground ginger
1 small teaspoon salt
4 eggs, room temperature
250g (8 oz) butter
250g (8 oz) castor sugar
125g (4 oz) glacé apricots,
cut into small pieces
60g (2 oz) glacé pineapple,
cut into small pieces
60g (2 oz) figs, cut into small pieces
60g (2 oz) crystallised ginger,
cut into small pieces
60g (2 oz) candied peel, cut into small pieces
125g (4 oz) glacé cherries,
cut into small pieces
60g (2 oz) almonds, cut into small pieces
250g (8 oz) butter, room temperature

Method

Preheat oven to 180° (350°F). Line a 20cm (7 in) square tin with greased foil. Put the glycerine, honey, marmalade, vanilla and almond essences, sherry and brandy into measuring jug. Sift flour 3 times with salt and ginger. Cream butter and sugar. Add eggs one at a time, then add the jug of essences and spirits, then add the fruit and nuts. Lastly add the dry ingredients. Pour into tin and bake in oven for 2 hours.

Val's diabetic fruit cake

Marie Miles, The Rock Show

Ingredients

3 cups mixed fruit
1 cup chopped walnuts
1 cup chopped dates
1 cup red wine
2 cups self-raising flour
$1/3$ cup milk
2 tablespoons vegetable oil
1 tablespoon bicarbonate soda
1 teaspoon mixed spice

Method

Preheat oven to 180°C (350°F). Lightly grease a 20cm (8 in) round cake tin. Line base and sides with baking paper.
In a large saucepan, combine mixed fruit, walnuts, dates, water and wine. Bring to boil and simmer for 3 minutes. Transfer to a large bowl and let cool for 10 minutes. Stir remaining ingredients into fruit mixture and combine well. Spoon into prepared tin.
Bake for 50–55 minutes, until cooked.
Cool cake in tin for 5 minutes. Turn out onto wire rack and cool completely.

Boiled fruit cake

Faye Amos, Cowra Show

Ingredients

125g (4 oz) butter
1 cup sugar
2 cups mixed fruit
1 teaspoon cinnamon
1 teaspoon mixed spice
1 teaspoon bicarbonate soda
1 cup cold water
2 eggs, beaten
1 cup self-raising flour
1 cup plain flour

Method

Preheat oven to 180°C (350°F).
Grease a 15cm
(6 in) square tin or 18cm (7 in) round tin.
In a large pot boil together butter, sugar,
mixed fruit, cinnamon, mixed spice,
bicarbonate soda and water. Let cool.
Add the eggs, self-raising flour and plain
flour and combine.
Cook for approximately 1 hour.

Rich fruit cake

Val Sloey, Bulahdelah Show

Val's mother passed this recipe on to Val when she married in 1955.

Ingredients

250g (8 oz) sultanas
250g (8 oz) currants
250g (8 oz) raisins
250g (8 oz) mixed fruit
125g (4 oz) cherries
125g (4 oz) mixed peel
¼ cup rum
50g flaked almonds
250g (8 oz) butter
250g (8 oz) brown sugar
1 tablespoon glycerine (to keep moist)
1 dessertspoon Parisian essence
1 dessertspoon coffee essence (for colour)
½ teaspoon cinnamon
½ teaspoon nutmeg
6 eggs
2 cups plain flour

Method

In a bowl mix together the sultanas, currants, raisins, mixed fruit, cherries and mixed peel. Pour over rum and let soak overnight. The next day, preheat oven to 150°C (300°F) or 120°C (250°F) fan forced. Line a ½ lb fruit cake tin or deep cake tin with baking paper. Add the flaked almonds to the fruit mixture. Cream together the butter and brown sugar, not too much, only until well combined. I do this on mixmaster or use a wooden spoon.

Then add the glycerine, Parisian essence, coffee, cinnamon, nutmeg and the eggs, one at a time, beating only until each is combined.

Lastly, stir in the flour; don't use the mixmaster, I use a wooden spoon, alternating with the fruit. Bake for approximately 3 hours. Test with skewer, I use a fine knitting needle.

Tip

Depress the mixture slightly in the centre of tin to approximately 2.5cm (1 in) from edges before cooking—this helps to make a flat top when cooked.

Honey roll

Ruby Lockyer, Glen Innes Show

Ingredients

3 eggs
½ cup sugar
½ cup cornflour
2 heaped teaspoons plain flour
1 level teaspoon cream of tartar
1 level teaspoon mixed spice
½ level teaspoon bicarbonate soda
½ level teaspoon cinnamon
1 level tablespoon melted honey

Method

Preheat oven to 180°C (350°F).
Grease a Swiss roll tin well.
Beat eggs for 3 minutes in a mixmaster.
Add sugar and beat until frothy and thick.
Sift flour and remaining dry ingredients
in a bowl. Add the egg and sugar mixture.
Hastily add the melted honey. Bake for 10–15
minutes. When ready, quickly roll in a slightly
damp cloth until cool. When cold, unroll,
spread with cream filling, then re-roll.

Cream filling

Ingredients

250ml (8 fl oz) cream
1–2 teaspoons honey, to taste

Method

In a small bowl, beat cream and honey
until thick.

Honey roll

Fudge cake

Margaret Williams, Newcastle Regional Show

Ingredients

1 tablespoon butter
¾ cup sugar
1 egg, well beaten
½ cup milk
1½ cups plain flour
1 teaspoon bicarbonate soda
2 teaspoons cream of tartar
Pinch salt
2 dessertspoons cocoa
½ cup boiling water

Method

Preheat oven to 180° (350°F). Grease a 18–20cm (7–8 in) shallow square or oblong tin. In a bowl, beat sugar and butter to a cream. Add egg and milk. Sift in all dry ingredients and beat well. Lastly add boiling water. Pour into cake tin and bake in oven for 30 minutes. Remove from oven and ice when cool.

Frosting

Ingredients

75g (2½ oz) butter, softened
2 tablespoons cocoa
1½ cups icing sugar
1 tablespoon milk

Method

Beat butter in a small bowl until smooth. Sift in the cocoa and icing sugar. Add milk and beat until smooth.

. . . .

Nut & date roll

Carla Goldman, Griffith Show

Carla has been exhibiting in the Griffith Show since she was 4 years old. At 13 she won Most Successful, Champion Cake in Junior Cookery and the trophy for Highest Pointscore in Junior Cookery. The next year she won 16 Years & Under Most Successful and the trophy for Highest Pointscore again. She also entered the Open Cookery section and won Most Successful Exhibitor (not previously achieved in the history of the Griffith Show). At 15 she repeated my success of the previous year in both the 16 Years & Under Junior Cooker, and the Open Cookery.

Ingredients

1 cup dates, chopped
1 teaspoon bicarbonate soda
1 cup boiling water
1 tablespoon butter
1 cup sugar
1 teaspoon vanilla essence
1 egg, well beaten
2 cups plain flour
1 teaspoon baking powder
½ cup walnuts

Method

Preheat oven to 160°C (320°F).
Grease 2 x roll tins.
Sprinkle soda onto chopped dates and add boiling water and let stand for 15 minutes. Combine sugar and butter and melt. Add to date mixture. Add egg, dry ingredients, nuts and vanilla essence. Place an equal amount of mixture into each tin. Stand tins up on a tray and bake in oven for approximately 30 minutes.

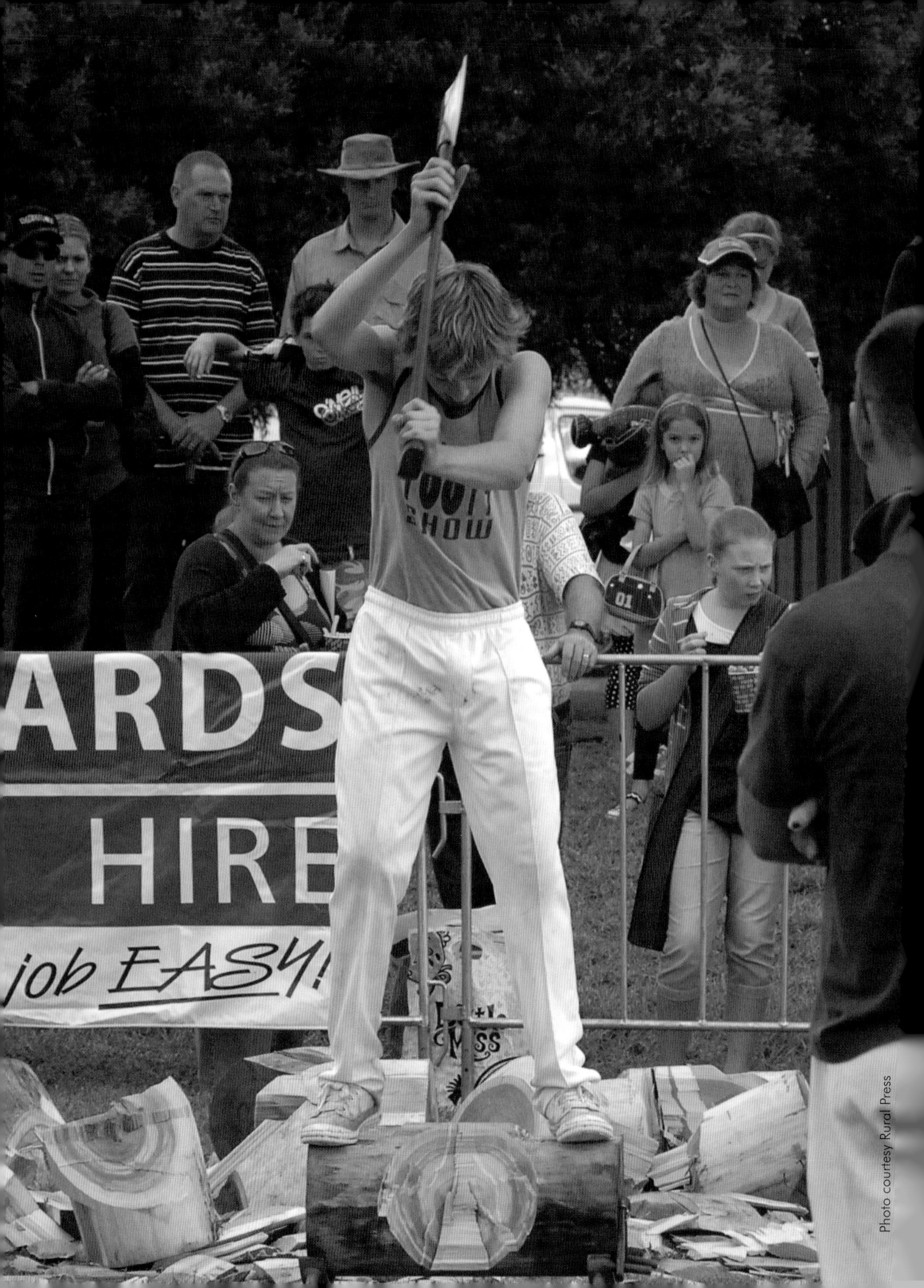

Photo courtesy Rural Press

· ·

Marble cake

Julie Bonanno, Albion Park Show

This cake has won many prizes over the last 20 years. It has been champion of the whole cooking section of Albion Park Show many times, as well as Dapto, Kiama, Berry and Nowra shows. It has also won at the Sydney Royal Easter Show and The Royal Melbourne Show.

Ingredients

125g (4 oz) butter, softened
1 scant cup (just under the measure)
of castor sugar
1 teaspoon vanilla
3 eggs
½ cup milk
1¾ cups self-raising flour
½ teaspoon baking powder
few drops cochineal
2 tablespoons cocoa

Method

Preheat oven to 170°C (330°F). Grease a round cake tin and line the bottom with baking paper. Beat butter and sugar until creamy and white. Add vanilla and then eggs, one at a time. Mix until well blended. Beat in milk. Sift flour and baking powder together well and mix into cream mixture until just blended. Divide mixture into three small bowls. In one of the bowls add the pink food colouring and mix until it is a pretty pink colour. Mix the cocoa with ¼ cup of boiling water and mix into the second bowl. Leave the third bowl plain. Place large spoonfuls of mixture in alternating colours into the tin. When all the mixture is used, swirl with a knife. Bake in oven for approximately 50 minutes and turn out immediately onto a cooling rack covered in a tea towel. Ice cake with pink icing.

Icing

Ingredients

2 cups icing sugar
2 tablespoons butter, soft
few drops cochineal

Method

Combine sugar and butter in a bowl and blend. Add teaspoon of hot water and conchineal and cream thoroughly until smooth.

· ·

Marble cake

Bev Clarke, Tumbarumba Show

Another marble cake recipe, this one with chocolate icing.

Ingredients

450g (1 lb) plain flour
2 teaspoons cream of tartar
1 teaspoon bicarbonate soda
225g (½ lb) butter
365g (¾ lb) sugar
4 eggs
1¼ cups of milk
1 tablespoon cocoa
1 teaspoon vanilla essence
1 teaspoon lemon essence
few drops cochineal

Method

Preheat oven to 180°C (350°F).
Grease a large 22cm (9 in) cake tin.
Sift flour, cream of tartar and bicarbonate soda together 3 times. In a bowl, cream butter and sugar until light and fluffy. Beat eggs into butter and sugar, one at a time. Fold in sieved flour mixture alternating with the milk a bit at a time. Divide mixture into 3 portions as follows: Mix cocoa with $1/3$ cup of hot water and add to the first portion.
Add cochineal and vanilla to the second portion. Add lemon essence to the remaining portion. Add spoonfuls of each cake mixture alternately to the cake tin until all are added. Do not mix them together just swirl gently with a knife to get the marble effect.
Bake for 45–50 minutes, or until an inserted skewer comes away clean.
Ice with chocolate icing.

Chocolate icing

Ingredients

100g cooking chocolate
1 tbsp butter
¼ cup cream

Method

Place cooking chocolate, butter and cream in a heatproof bowl. Bring a small quantity of water to the boil in a saucepan, remove from the heat and place the bowl of chocolate on top. Stir until the chocolate melts and the mixture is well blended.
Remove from the heat and cool until the mixture begins to thicken.

· ·

Tea cake

Pat Rodd, Tumut Show

Ingredients

1 cup cream
1 cup sugar
2 eggs
1 teaspoon vanilla essence
1½ cups self-raising flour

Method

Preheat oven to 180°C (350°F).
Grease a loaf tin.
Beat cream and sugar together. Add eggs and vanilla and fold in self-raising flour. Pour into tin and cook in oven for 45 minutes.
Remove from oven, spread with butter and sprinkle with sugar and vanilla. Eat while hot.

. . . .

Rainbow cake

Lorna Knapp, Berry Show

Ingredients

225g (½ lb) butter
450g (1 lb) sugar
6 eggs
1 small cup (approx 237ml) of milk
450g (1 lb) plain flour
2 teaspoons cream of tartar
1 teaspoon bicarbonate soda
1 teaspoon lemon essence
few drops
1 teaspoon vanilla essence
2½ tablespoons cocoa

Method

Preheat oven to 180°C (350°F).
Grease a 20cm (8 in) tin.
Cream butter and sugar well. Add eggs, one at a time, then milk. Add well sifted flour, cream of tartar and bicarbonate soda. Mix well. Divide mixture into three equal parts. Flavour one part with essence of lemon and colour with cochineal. Flavour another part with vanilla and colour with cocoa, mixed with a small amount of water. Leave one part plain. Carefully pour each mixture in, one-by-one and cook in oven for approximately 45 minutes.

Icing

Ingredients

28g (1 oz) butter, soft
125g (4 oz) cream cheese, soft
2–3 cups icing sugar
1 dessertspoon milk

Method

Mix butter, cheese and 2½ cups icing sugar together until the mixture is smooth and holds a peak. Add milk and more icing sugar, if required, to get a spreadable but not sloppy consistency.

Rainbow cake

· ·

Orange delight cake

Audrey Somers, Parkes Show

Audrey has been cooking for the Parkes show for more than 60 years, this is one of her favourite cakes, easy to make and very tasty.

Ingredients

250g (8 oz) butter or substitute
1 cup of sugar
2 eggs
1¾ cups plain flour
1 teaspoon baking powder
½ teaspoon bicarbonate soda
½ teaspoon salt
⅓ cup of milk
1 cup chopped raisins, chopped
½ cup chopped walnuts, chopped
1 teaspoon grated orange rind
½ cup orange juice
⅓ cup sugar extra

Method

Preheat oven to 180°C (350°F).
Grease a 23cm x 12cm (9 in x 5 in) loaf tin and line with baking paper.
Cream butter and sugar together. Add eggs, one at a time, beating well after each addition. Fold in sifted dry ingredients alternately with the milk. Fold in raisins, walnuts and orange rind and mix well.
Place mixture in tin and bake for 1 hour, or until cooked when tested.
Put extra sugar and orange juice in a saucepan, stir over gentle heat until sugar is dissolved. While cake is still hot remove from tin, place on oven tray and spoon syrup over.

· ·

Orange butter cake

Sarah Wray, Penrith Show

Ingredients

125g (4 oz) butter
¾ cup castor sugar
grated rind of 2 oranges
2 eggs
1½ cups self-raising flour
¼ cup orange juice
¼ cup milk
¼ cup orange marmalade, to serve

Method

Preheat oven to 180°C (350°F).
Grease a loaf tin.
Cream butter, sugar and grated orange rind
until light and fluffy. Add eggs, one at a time,
beating well after each one. Fold through
sifted flour and, when thoroughly mixed,
gently stir through the orange juice and milk.
Bake for about 50 minutes. Test with a
skewer before removing from oven. Stand for
a few minutes before removing from tin. Pour
orange marmalade over the hot cake and
allow to cool.

Shirley's orange cake

Shirley Thompson, Ashford Show

Ingredients

125g (4 oz) butter
¾ cup castor sugar
1 tablespoon orange juice
rind of 1 orange
2 eggs, beaten
small ½ cup milk
1¾ cups self-raising flour
2 tablespoons cold water

Method

Preheat oven to 180°C (350°F).
Grease an 18cm (7 in) round tin.
Cream butter and sugar together. Add orange juice and orange rind and mix. Then add eggs, milk and flour. Add water last. Bake in oven for 30–40 minutes.

Orange cake

Judy Henderson, Mendooran Show

This orange cake recipe has been a favourite in Judy's family for many years. She says it is a lovely moist cake and has won first prize and overall champion cake several times.

Ingredients

150g (5 oz) margarine
1 cup castor sugar
2 small eggs
grated rind of 1 orange
pinch of salt
½ cup of milk
1½ cups self-raising flour
¼ cup boiling water

Method

Preheat oven to 180°C (350°F).
Grease and line a loaf tin.
Cream margarine and sugar together.
Add eggs, one at a time, then orange rind.
Add salt then half of the milk (¼ cup).
Add three-quarters of the flour, the remainder of the milk, then the remaining flour and mix well.
Lastly add the hot water.
Bake in oven for 40 minutes, or until cooked.

Orange cake

· ·

Orange cake

Thelma Allman, Kiama Show

Ingredients

140g (4½ oz) butter
1 cup sugar
3 eggs
2 cups self-raising flour
¾ cup milk
Juice and rind of 1 orange

Method

Preheat oven to 180°C (350°F).
Grease a 20cm (8 in) tin. Cream butter with
sugar. Add eggs one at a time, beating well
after each one. Fold in flour alternately with
milk. Lastly fold in orange juice and rind.
Bake for approximately 40 minutes or until
cake is 'quiet', i.e. has stopped bubbling
inside. Remove from oven and let cool.
Turn out onto a cake rack and ice.

Orange icing

Ingredients

2 cups icing sugar
2 tablespoons butter, soft
juice of ½ orange

Method

Combine butter and icing sugar in a bowl.
Add enough lemon juice to make a soft paste
and mix well.

. . . .

Peach blossom cake

Morna Wilson, Gloucester Show

It is a thrill to be a prize winner in any competition, but there is nothing better than the pride in winning a Blue Ribbon at the Sydney Royal with this cake. Just the pinnacle of achievement for me!

Ingredients

125g (4 oz) butter or margarine
1 cup castor sugar
½ cup milk
1 cup plain flour
1 teaspoon baking powder
½ cup wheaten cornflour
4 eggwhites

Method

Preheat oven to 180ºC (350ºF).
Grease and flour a 20cm (8 in) round tin
Beat butter and sugar until light and creamy. Add sifted dry ingredients and milk alternatively. Lastly add stiffly beaten eggwhites. Fold through gently.
Place half the mixture in another bowl and colour a very light pink. Put alternate spoonfuls of the two mixtures into the tin. When all mixture is used, swirl the two colours together slightly with a skewer. Bake for 40–45 minutes, or until cooked. Cool completely. Ice sides of cake with very pale pink icing.

Icing

Ingredients

2 cups icing sugar
2 tablespoons butter, soft
drop cochineal

Method

Combine sugar and butter in a bowl and blend. Add teaspoon of hot water and conchineal and cream thoroughly until smooth.

Passionfruit sandwich

Liz Brook, Milton Show

Ingredients

250g (8 oz) butter
2 cups castor sugar
2 teaspoons vanilla
4 eggs
3 cups plain flour
½ teaspoon salt
3 teaspoons baking powder
1 cup milk

Method

Preheat oven to 180° (350°F). Grease 2 x 20cm (8 in) sandwich tins.
Beat butter, sugar and vanilla together until light and creamy. Add eggs, one at a time. Fold in dry ingredients alternately with the milk. Beat mixture lightly until smooth.
Pour into tins and bake for 35 minutes. When cold, join together with mock cream and ice with passionfruit icing.

Mock cream

Ingredients

2 cups sugar
1 cup butter
1–2 tablespoons passionfruit pulp, to taste

Method

In a small bowl, cream butter and sugar together well until light in colour. Add passionfruit and mix well.

Passionfruit icing

Ingredients

2 cups icing sugar
2 tablespoons butter, soft
pulp of 2–3 passionfruit, depending on size

Method

Combine sugar, butter and passionfruit pulp in a saucepan and stir over low heat until a smooth consistency. Cool slightly and pour over cake.

· ·

Patty cakes

Yvonne Maslin, Albion Park Show

These patty cakes have won at Albion Park show nearly every year since Yvonne began cooking 28 years ago. They also were victorious at The Royal Easter Show in the early 1990s in a highly contested section of 27 entries where they were described as 'the perfect patty cake' by the CWA judge. She usually ices them with a very pale pink icing but her son Kieren (who is 13) baked this recipe for the 2009 Albion Park Show in the junior cooking section and iced them a pale green colour much to my disgust but managed to win champion junior exhibit. The recipe is that good!

Ingredients

125g (4 oz) butter, softened
1 cup castor sugar
3 eggs
½ cup milk
1¼ cups self-raising flour
½ cup cornflour

Method

Preheat oven to 220°C (425°F).
Grease patty cake tin well, I find this better than using patty cake papers.
Beat butter and sugar until well blended and creamy. Add eggs, one at a time, and beat well after each addition. Add milk and then flours, which have been sifted together 3 times. Beat until just combined. Divide mix into patty cake tin and fill each ⅔ full. Bake 12–15 minutes or until they spring back when touched lightly. Turn onto covered cooling rack and cool before icing.

Icing

Ingredients

2 cups icing sugar
2 tablespoons butter, soft
drop cochineal

Method

Combine sugar and butter in a bowl and blend. Add teaspoon of hot water and conchineal and cream thoroughly until smooth.

Makes approximately 2 dozen

· ·

Rock cakes

Helen Wotton, Morisset/Lake Macquarie Show

Ingredients

2 cups self-raising flour
$1/3$ cup raw sugar
½ teaspoon cinnamon
90g (3 oz) unsalted butter, melted
$2/3$ cup currants
¼ cup mixed peel
$1/3$–½ cup milk
1 egg, beaten

Method

Preheat oven to 180° (350°F).
Place dry ingredients in a bowl. Pour over melted butter with a fork and add currants and peel. Mix well. Add the egg and then sufficient milk until mixture resembles scone mix. Place a teaspoon of mixture on a greased oven tray. Sprinkle with a little raw sugar and bake for 10–15 minutes. Whilst hot loosen on the tray and leave to cool. Enjoy.

Lamingtons

Norma Cleal, Warialda Show

Ingredients

225g (½ lb) butter, soft
1½ cups sugar
2 cups self-raising flour
2 tablespoons cornflour
1 teaspoon baking powder
pinch salt
½ cup milk (a little more may be needed)
4 eggs
lemon juice or essence
1 teaspoon vanilla

Method

Preheat oven to 180°C (350°F).
Grease a large lamington tin.
Sift flours, baking powder and salt together.
Put all ingredients in a large bowl and beat
for 5–6 minutes. Pour into tin and bake in
oven for 50–60 minutes, or until cooked. Cool
then deep freeze for two days.

Icing

Ingredients

90g (3 oz) butter
1 tablespoon cocoa
250g (8 oz) icing sugar
1 teaspoon vanilla

Method

In a large bowl, combine all the ingredients.
Add hot water, a little at a time, to make
mixture runny.

To make up

A large bowl or plate of coconut

Method

Remove cake from freezer and cut into
5cm (2 in) squares. Dip each square into the
hot icing bowl using a fork. Roll in coconut
and pat into shape. Keep frozen.

Makes a good dozen lamingtons

Lamingtons

. . . .

Queen Elizabeth cake

Margaret Barron, Cooma Show

Ingredients

1 cup dates, chopped
1 cup boiling water
1 cup sugar
1 teaspoon vanilla
¼ cup butter
1 egg beaten
1 ½ cups plain flour
1 teaspoon baking powder
1 teaspoon bicarbonate soda

Method

Preheat oven to 180°C (350°F).
Grease a 22cm (9 in) square tin for a flatter cake or round tin for a higher cake.
Put dates in a bowl and pour over water. Add sugar, vanilla and butter and stir until butter has melted and sugar dissolved. Add egg, flour, baking powder, bicarbonate soda and mix well. Bake for 45 minutes. While it is cooking make the topping.

Topping

Ingredients

1 cup coconut
8 tablespoons brown sugar
3 tablespoons cream
5 tablespoons butter

Method

Put all ingredients in saucepan and cook over low heat until melted and well mixed.

. . . .

Ginger fluff

Annie Swanson, Tullamore Show

This recipe, submitted by Annie's daughter Margaret McAneney, is one of her prize-winning entries in the cookery section. She has long since passed away but was a keen exhibitor all her life. Her ginger fluff won many prizes over the years in the local show.

Ingredients

4 eggs, separated
¾ cup sugar
1 dessertspoon golden syrup
½ cup arrowroot or cornflour
2 dessertspoons plain flour
1 teaspoon ground ginger
1 teaspoon baking powder
1 teaspoon cocoa
1 teaspoon cinnamon

Method

Preheat oven to 200°C (400°F).
Beat eggwhites, add sugar gradually, then the yolks. Add syrup and beat until fluffy. Sift the dry ingredients together at least 4 times. Fold into mixture with a spoon. Pour into sponge tin and bake for 20 minutes.

Parsnip, pecan & cinnamon cake

Joy Schultz, The Rock Show

Ingredients

375g (12 oz) parsnip, grated
125g (4 oz) loosely packed brown sugar
250g (8 oz) castor sugar
1 cup extra light olive oil or peanut oil
3 eggs
¼ teaspoon vanilla essence
¾ cup pecans, chopped
2 teaspoon ground cinnamon
125g (4 oz) self-raising flour
icing sugar, to dust
mascarpone, to serve

Method

Preheat oven to 180ºC (350ºF) or 160ºC (320ºF) fan forced. Grease a wide loaf tin and line base with baking paper.
Combine parsnip, brown sugar, castor sugar and flour in a bowl.
Combine oil, eggs and vanilla in a separate bowl and whisk until smooth. Add to parsnip mixture and stir well. Add pecans and cinnamon. Pour into tin and bake for 1 hour or until a skewer comes out clean. Set tin on rack to cool. Turn out and dust with icing sugar. Serve in slices with mascarpone.

. . . .

Pumpkin fruit cake

Sharon Mason, Grafton Show

Ingredients

1 tablespoon butter
1 cup sugar
2 eggs
1 tablespoon golden syrup
1 cup cold mashed pumpkin
1 tablespoon vanilla
2 teaspoons coffee extract
1 teaspoon cinnamon
1 teaspoon spice
pinch of nutmeg and clove
500g (1 lb) assorted mixed dried fruits
and nuts if liked
2 large cups self-raising flour

Method

Preheat oven to 180°C (350°F).
Grease and line a 20cm (8 in) cake tin.
Cream butter and sugar together. Add eggs
and beat well. Add rest of the ingredients in
order. Lastly, sift in the flour and mix well.
Bake for about 2 hours.

Pumpkin fruit cake

Rene Clark Weethalle Show

Ingredients

450g (1 lb) butter
2 cups sugar
4 eggs
4 cups plain flour
2 cups mashed pumpkin, cold
1 cup mixed fruit
1½ teaspoons baking powder (added to flour)

Method

Preheat oven to 150°C (300°F).
Grease a 22cm (9 in) square tin.
Combine flour, pumpkin and fruit in a bowl.
Cream butter and sugar together. Add eggs, one at a time, alternating with about ¼ of the flour mixture. Pour into tin and cook in oven for 1½–2 hours.

· ·

Pumpkin & sultana cake

Glen Innes Show

Ingredients

2 cups sultanas
50ml (1¾ fl oz) honey
200ml orange juice
1 teaspoon bicarbonate soda
2 cups self-raising wholemeal flour
1 teaspoon cinnamon
1 teaspoon powdered ginger
2 eggs
1 teaspoon vanilla
2 tablespoons brown sugar
1 cup mashed pumpkin
¹/₃ cup chopped pecans

Method

Preheat oven to 170°C (325°F).
Grease and line a 20cm (8 in) square cake tin.
In a saucepan place sultanas, honey, orange juice and bicarbonate soda and bring to the boil. Sift in flour, cinnamon and ginger. Mix together eggs, vanilla and brown sugar and add to mixture. Add the pumpkin and pecans and combine. Place mixture into cake tin and bake for approximately 1½ hours.

· ·

Sultana cake

Beris Jakins, Mungindi Show

This is an old recipe handed down from Beris's mum who came by it while watching a TV cooking show in the early 1960s. The sultanas for this recipe need to be prepared the day before baking.

Ingredients

750g (1½ lb) sultanas
250g (½ lb) butter
250g (½ lb) sugar
4 large eggs
300g (10 oz) plain flour
60g (2 oz) self-raising flour
125g (4 oz) chopped almonds
2 tablespoons brandy
1 teaspoon vanilla

Method

Preheat oven to 150°C (300°F). Grease and line a 19cm x 19cm (7½ in x 7½ in) tin. Soak sultanas in warm water in a saucepan for 2 hours. Drain in a colander for 12 hours or overnight.
Cream butter and sugar together. Beat eggs, one at a time, into creamed mixture. Sift both flours, add sultanas and almonds alternatively with flour. Lastly add brandy and vanilla. Spoon mixture into tin and bake in oven for 1½–2 hours.

· ·

Sultana cake

Ann Garard, Kiama Show

Ingredients

250g (8 oz) butter
250g (8 oz) castor sugar
4 eggs
500g (1 lb) sultanas
1½ cups plain flour
½ cup self-raising flour
pinch salt
1 teaspoon lemon essence or lemon juice
1 teaspoon vanilla essence

Method

Preheat oven to 170°C (330°F). Prepare a deep 20cm x 7cm (8 in x 2.5 in) tin. Line inside with baking paper and wrap outside with brown paper. Cream butter and sugar until light and creamy. Break each egg into a cup and add one at a time, folding in each one. Sift flours and salt together, reserving a small amount to coat sultanas, and add flour to egg, butter, sugar mix. Add essences. Mix reserved flour through sultanas until coated. Fold into batter until completely mixed. Pour into greased tin making sure there are no gaps. Smooth top with wet hand. Bake in oven for approximately 2 hours. Place tin on thick magazine on oven shelf. Cover top loosely with foil if browning too quickly. Allow to cool in tin.

Brandied sultana cake

Virginia (Vinnie) Hall, Rylstone-Kandos Show

This sultana cake recipe has brandy for an extra kick.

Ingredients

250g (8 oz) butter
1 cup castor sugar
5 eggs
2½ cups plain flour
¼ cup self-raising flour
¼ cup brandy
750g (1½ lb) sultanas

Method

Cover sultanas with warm water and let stand 2 hours. Drain well. Place on tray covered with absorbent paper, stand overnight to dry. The next day, preheat oven to 160°C (325°F). Grease a deep 23cm (9 in) round or 20cm (8 in) square cake tin and line base and sides with paper. Cream butter and sugar in a large bowl with electric mixer until just combined. Add eggs quickly, one at a time, and beat until combined. Stir in half the sifted flours with half the brandy and half the sultanas, then stir in remaining flours, brandy and sultanas. Spread mixture into prepared tin. Bake in oven for about 2 hours. Cover cake with a tea towel and cool in the tin.

. . . .

Twelfth night cake

Julie Mutton, Ariah Park Show

The fruit in this recipe needs to be soaked in sherry and brandy overnight before putting in mixture.

Ingredients

$^1/_3$ cup sliced glacé cherries
½ cup sultanas
$^1/_3$ cup finely chopped apricots (optional)
1 tablespoon sherry
1 tablespoon brandy
250g (8 oz) butter
1 teaspoon vanilla essence
1 cup castor sugar
4 eggs
1 cup ground almonds (optional)
1 cup plain flour
¾ cup self-raising flour
½ teaspoon ground cinnamon
¼ cup milk

Method

The day before making, place the fruit, sherry and brandy in a bowl and soak overnight.
The next day, preheat oven to150°C (300°F). Grease a deep 20cm (8 in) round cake tin, line base with paper and grease paper.
Beat butter, vanilla and sugar in small bowl with electric mixer until light and fluffy. Add eggs, one at a time, beating well between additions. Transfer mixture to large bowl, stir in fruit and nuts, then sifted dry ingredients alternating with milk.
Spread mixture into prepared tin and bake in oven for about 2 hours. When cooked, cover with foil and cool in tin.
When cake is cooked pour topping over it and return to oven for 2 minutes or until set.

Puddings, pies & tarts

Photo courtesy Rural Press

Boiled fruit pudding

Reta Spencer, Barellan Show

Ingredients

250g (8 oz) butter
250g (8 oz) brown sugar
5 small eggs
250g (8 oz) raisins
250g (8 oz) sultanas
250g (8 oz) mixed peel
125g (4 oz) currants
5 tablespoons rum
125g (4 oz) plain flour
pinch salt
1 teaspoon mixed spice
½ teaspoon nutmeg
½ teaspoon bicarbonate soda
125g (4 oz) breadcrumbs, rubbed fine

Method

Cream butter and sugar together in a bowl. Add eggs, one at a time, beating well after each addition. Stir in the fruit and rum. Stir flour with salt, mixed spice, nutmeg and bicarbonate soda and add to mixture together with breadcrumbs and mix well.

Put mixture into a pudding cloth and fasten tightly with string. Bring a large pot of water to a rapid boil. Place pudding into the boiling water and continue boiling steadily for 4½ hours. Add more boiling water as necessary to keep it covered. Remove from water as soon as cooking time is complete and turn out immediately onto a plate.

Boiled plum pudding

Elaine Buckley, Peak Hill Show

Here is another variation on boiled pudding. This recipe has been handed down from Elaine's mother-in-law's family and is an Easter and Christmas day special. It has won many prizes including 1st prize at the Peak Hill Show for 37 years, Champion of Show three times as well as at state level. The fruit needs to soak for several days, so start this one well ahead of time.

Ingredients

1250g (2½ lb) mixed fruit such as currants, sultanas, raisins and dates
225g (½ lb) butter
225g (½ lb) brown sugar
6 eggs
2½–3 cups self-raising flour
½ cup breadcrumbs
¼ cup boiling water
½ teaspoon bicarbonate soda
½ teaspoon each mixed spice, ginger, nutmeg, cinnamon
pinch of salt
1 teaspoon vanilla
rum, to taste
brandy, to taste
sherry, to taste

Method

Cut larger fruit to size of currants and soak in sweet sherry for at least 3–4 days.
When the fruit is ready, cream butter and brown sugar. Add eggs, one at a time. Then alternately add the sifted flour, salt and spices, fruit and breadcrumbs. Dissolve the bicarbonate soda in the boiling water and add. Add rum, brandy to taste.
Tie firmly in a floured calico cloth.
Bring a large pot of water to the boil. Place a plate in the bottom to stop the pudding sticking to the pot and place the pudding in it for 5–5½ hours. Do not let the pot go off the boil and add boiling water when needed.
When cooked, remove from still boiling water.
Can be turned out or left hanging until needed.

. . . .

Family-size plum pudding

Barbara Carter, Dorrigo Show

This plum pudding has also won first prize on many occasions and has won Champion exhibit in the cooking section three times.

Ingredients

450g (1 lb) raisins
450g (1 lb) sultanas
450g (1 lb) currants
1½ cups wine, port or rum
450g (1 lb) butter
450g (1 lb) brown sugar
8–10 eggs
450g (1 lb) plain flour
4 cups breadcrumbs
2 tablespoons spice
1 teaspoon bicarbonate soda
1 packet glacé cherries
½ cup walnuts

Method

Finely chop fruit, pour wine over and leave to soak overnight.
Cream butter and sugar. Add eggs, one at a time. Add sifted flour and other dry ingredients, a small amount at a time, alternating with the fruit. Boil in cloth for 4–5 hours. Allow to cool, overnight, reboil 1–1½ hours, remove cloth while hot.
To prepare cloth (approximately 1 metre/39 in square): wet thoroughly in very hot water, squeeze out and flour well. Place cloth in container and spoon pudding mixture into it. Tie top tightly with cooking string. Place pudding into large boiler of boiling water with a saucer on the bottom to prevent pudding sticking. Keep water boiling all the time during cooking.

. . . .

Rich plum pudding steamed in a cloth

Gwen Brown, Lake Cargelligo Show

This recipe was taken from Gwen's grandmother's old recipe book. She says: 'I have used this recipe for over thirty years for our Christmas Pudding. I have entered it in our Lake Cargelligo Show over a long period of years, winning First Prize and Champion ribbons many times.'

Ingredients

1kg (2 lb) dried fruit including raisins, sultanas, dates and currants, chopped
¼ cup of chopped almonds
4½ cups of soft white breadcrumbs
1½ cups self-raising flour
4 eggs, beaten
1 cup butter or margarine
1¼ cups brown sugar (can use castor sugar)
5 tablespoons brandy, whisky or rum
juice of 1 lemon plus the grated rind

Method

Place fruit, nuts, lemon rind in a basin, pour spirits over and leave overnight.
In a large bowl, put breadcrumbs, sifted flour and spice, and rub in softened margarine/butter. Add fruit, eggs and lemon juice and mix well. Mixture should be good dropping consistency; if too stiff, add a little milk, if too runny, add a little flour and mix well.
Have ready a large boiler ⅔ full of rapidly boiling water. Place a bread and butter plate or saucer in the bottom of the boiler so the pudding does not touch bottom. Lower pudding into boiling water. Cook for 5–6 hours, making sure the water does not go off the boil. Every hour add more boiling water—it must remain covered with water and boiling the whole time.

continued ...

. . . .

To serve

Pudding may be removed from cloth as directed below.
If planning to leave pudding in cloth until needed, hang by the string in a cool, dry,
airy place such as a pantry.
On the day of serving, return pudding to boiling water and boil for 2 hours.
Remove pudding from water and place in a colander, cut string and remove.
Peel cloth back carefully, remove circle of greaseproof paper. Place a dinner plate on top of the
pudding, holding both plate and colander, turn over so plate is underneath, remove colander
and peel off cloth. Pudding is ready to serve or can be wrapped in a freezer bag and stored in
the fridge or deep freeze.

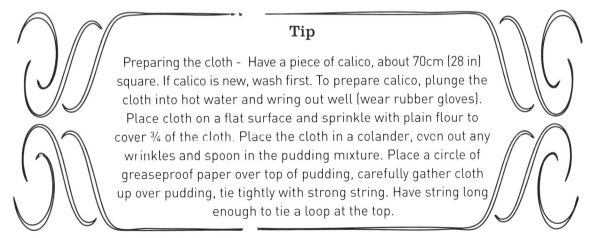

Tip

Preparing the cloth - Have a piece of calico, about 70cm (28 in)
square. If calico is new, wash first. To prepare calico, plunge the
cloth into hot water and wring out well (wear rubber gloves).
Place cloth on a flat surface and sprinkle with plain flour to
cover ¾ of the cloth. Place the cloth in a colander, even out any
wrinkles and spoon in the pudding mixture. Place a circle of
greaseproof paper over top of pudding, carefully gather cloth
up over pudding, tie tightly with strong string. Have string long
enough to tie a loop at the top.

. . . .

Passionfruit delicious pudding

Esme McRae, Armidale and New England Show

Ingredients

3 eggs, separated
¾ cup sugar
1 cup crushed pineapple
1 tablespoon flour
pulp of 2 passionfruit
salt
extra ½ cup of sugar

Method

Preheat oven to 160°C (320°F). Beat egg yolks with sugar. Beat in pineapple, flour, passionfruit pulp and salt.
In a separate bowl, beat eggwhites with extra sugar. Fold into passionfruit mixture.
Pour into a pudding dish to bake. Fill a pan with cold water and place the pudding bowl in this to stop it boiling. Place in oven and cook for 50–60 minutes.

Passionfruit
delicious pudding

. . . .

Apple pie

Wendy Cleve, Berrigan Show

Filling

Ingredients

10 green apples, peeled and sliced
3 tablespoons sugar
¼ cup water
½ dozen cloves

Method

Place apples, sugar, water and cloves in a large saucepan and boil, with the lid on, until apples are tender. Take the lid off and continue to cook on low for approximately 10 minutes, until the liquid dries. Set aside while you make the pastry.

Pastry

Ingredients

2 cups plain flour
1 teaspoon baking powder
2 tablespoons castor sugar
170g (6 oz) butter

Method

Preheat oven to 180°C (350°F) or 160°C (325°F) fan-forced). Combine the flour, baking powder and castor sugar in a bowl. Rub butter into dry ingredients a little at a time. Slowly add 125ml (4 fl oz) of cold water, bit by bit. When the dough is combined, roll out 2 sheets onto a floured board. Line pie plate with pastry, add apple and put second sheet of pastry on top. Glaze with sugar and water and sprinkle with sugar. Cook in oven for 40 minutes.

· ·

Apple pie

L Weaver, Batlow Show

Batlow is famous for apples and so of course we had to include an apple pie recipe from there.

Ingredients

½ block (125g) of cooking margarine, softened
½ cup of sugar
1 egg
1 cup self-raising flour
1 cup plain flour
4–5 Granny Smith apples, peeled, cored and sliced
extra sugar for stewing apples

Method

Preheat oven to 180°C (350°F).
Cream the cooking margarine with the sugar. Add the egg. Stir in the self-raising flour, then stir in the plain flour. Roll between two sheets of greaseproof paper. Line the bottom of your pie plate and blind bake.
To stew the apples, wash and place in a small saucepan with a small amount of sugar to taste.There should be enough water on the apple slices to cook until tender. If not, add 1 tablespoon of water. Use cloves if desired.
Fill pie case, cover, and bake for 30 minutes or until cooked.

Lemon meringue cream dessert

May Harris, Nambucca River Show

Meringue

Ingredients

4 eggwhites
1¼ cups castor sugar
1 teaspoon lemon juice
2 teaspoons icing sugar
cornflour for dusting

Method

Preheat oven to 100°C (200°F). Cut a 25cm (10 in) circle from a piece of greaseproof paper. Place on lightly greased oven tray. Brush paper with melted butter, dust with cornflour and shake off excess cornflour. Combine eggwhites, castor sugar and lemon juice in small basin of electric mixer, and beat on high speed for 15 minutes. Fold in sifted icing sugar. Spread a 7mm layer of meringue over the prepared greaseproof paper. Pipe remaining meringue mixture around edge to form shell. Bake in oven for 1–1.5 hours, or until dry to touch. Cool in oven with door ajar. Remove paper from meringue and place on serving plate.

Filling

Ingredients

¹/₃ cup cornflour
½ cup sugar
1 cup water
2 teaspoons grated lemon rind
¹/₃ cup lemon juice
30g (1 oz) butter
4 egg yolks
½ cup thickened cream

Method

Heat a frying pan on the stovetop and blend cornflour and sugar with water, lemon rind and lemon juice, stirring constantly until mixture boils and thickens. Reduce heat and simmer, stirring, for 1 minute. Remove from heat, stir in butter and egg yolks, then cover and let cool to room temperature. Stir in cream. Spread filling into meringue shell and refrigerate until set. Decorate with whipped cream and fruit.

Note: if not ready to spread, press a piece of plastic food wrap onto surface of filling to prevent skin forming.

· ·

Pavlova

Wilma Bott, Barellan Show

Ingredients

4 eggwhites
1 cup castor sugar
1 teaspoon lemon juice
¼ cup sugar
1 tablespoon cornflour

Method

Preheat oven to 150°C (300°F).
Beat eggwhites until soft peaks form.
Gradually add castor sugar, beating until dissolved and mixture is thick.
Add the lemon juice, sugar and cornflour and beat on low into the meringue. Place sheet of baking paper on tray and make a circle with mixture to approximately 23cm (9 in). With a spatula work around the circle lifting as you go to make ridge around the pavlova. Bake in oven for 50 minutes. Leave in oven to go cold. When ready to serve, fill with cream and fruit of your choice.

Tip

When finished baking, leave the meringue in the oven, with door ajar, to cool completely. If you remove the meringue when it's still warm it will cool too quickly and may crack or collapse.

Pavlova

. . . .

Custard tart

George Williams, Hawkesbury Show

This recipe was submitted by Lyn Williams on behalf of her late husband, George. She says it was never been beaten in any show he entered it in.

Filling

Ingredients

½ cup milk
4 eggs, slightly beaten
½ cup sugar
¼ teaspoon salt
½ teaspoon vanilla
45 cm (18 in) pie shell, unbaked
nutmeg, to decorate

Method

Preheat oven to 200°C (400°F).
Scald milk by heating in a saucepan until small bubbles appear. Blend eggs, sugar, salt and vanilla and gradually stir into the scalded milk. Leave to cool. Sprinkle nutmeg on top.

Sweet shortcrust pastry

Ingredients

1¾ cups plain flour
2 tablespoons self-raising flour
¼ teaspoon salt
$1/3$ cup castor sugar
150g (5 oz) shortening
1 egg, slightly beaten

Method

Sift the plain flour, self-raising flour and salt together into a bowl, then add sugar. Rub in shortening, until it resembles the texture of breadcrumbs. Add the egg. Roll to fit a 20cm (8 in) pie dish. Slightly prick base and sides of pastry. Pour the custard into the pie shell. Sprinkle with nutmeg and bake in oven for 25–30 minutes.

Custard tart

· ·

Pineapple chiffon tart

Yvonne Maslin, Ariah Park Show

Pastry

Ingredients

90g (3 oz) margarine
60g (2 oz) sugar
1 egg
60g (2 oz) plain flour
60g (2 oz) self-raising flour
30g (1 oz) cornflour

Method

Preheat oven to 180°C (350°F).
Cream margarine and sugar together,
add egg and beat well. Sift the flours together
four times and work into creamed mixture.
Line pie plate and blind bake for
10–15 minutes.

Filling

Ingredients

1 x 450g tin crushed pineapple
1 cup water
1 pineapple jelly mix
2 heaped tablespoons milk powder

Method

Drain pineapple and set aside juice and fruit
in separate bowls. Place pineapple juice and
jelly crystals into a saucepan and heat until
jelly is dissolved. Allow to cool. Mix milk
powder and water, beat in the jelly mixture
and finally fold in crushed pineapple. Spoon
into pie shell and place in fridge to set. Serve
with whipped cream or ice cream.

· ·

Savoury pie

Irene Murat, Ardlethan Show

Ingredients

1 tablespoon flour
1 dessertspoon butter
1 cup milk
1 tomato, peeled and chopped
salt and pepper
1 cup grated cheese
2 eggs, well beaten
½ cup bacon, chopped
1 onion, finely chopped

Method

Preheat oven to 180°C (350°F).
Place flour, butter and milk in a saucepan and heat. Add remaining ingredients and mix well. Place in uncooked pastry shell and bake in oven for 25 minutes.

Biscuits
& slices

Brown butter biscuits

Phil Fisher, Kiama Show

Ingredients

115g (¼ lb) butter
½ cup sugar
1 egg, beaten
1 teaspoon vanilla
1¼ cups self-raising flour
pinch salt
170g (6 oz) almonds

Method

Preheat oven to 180° (350°F).
Butter a baking tray.
Melt butter (cool lightly), add sugar and beat lightly. Stir in egg, vanilla and fold in flour and salt. Roll into little balls. Place on tray and flatten with a fork, allowing room to spread. Place an almond on top of each and press with fork.
Bake in oven for 10–12 minutes.

Makes 20 biscuits

Tip

Don't crowd biscuits on the tray—air needs to circulate around them for even cooking. Place biscuit dough in rows, lining up each row to sit behind the gaps formed by the biscuits in front.

. . . .

Pecan biscuits

Heidi Channell, Picton Show

Ingredients

125g (4 oz) pecans, halved
60g (2 oz) butter
¼ cup icing sugar
1 teaspoon of vanilla
½ cup plain flour

Method

Preheat oven to 180°C (350°F).
Lightly grease an oven or baking tray.
Finely chop a quarter of the nuts, reserving the remainder. Cream butter with sifted icing sugar and vanilla until light and fluffy. Add the pecan and stir in sifted flour in two lots. Use floured hands to roll level teaspoons of mixture into balls. Place balls 2.5cm (1 in) apart on tray. Place a pecan half on each ball. Bake in oven for 10 minutes, or until light golden brown. Cool on tray. Dust with icing sugar before serving.

Makes 18 biscuits

Anzac biscuits

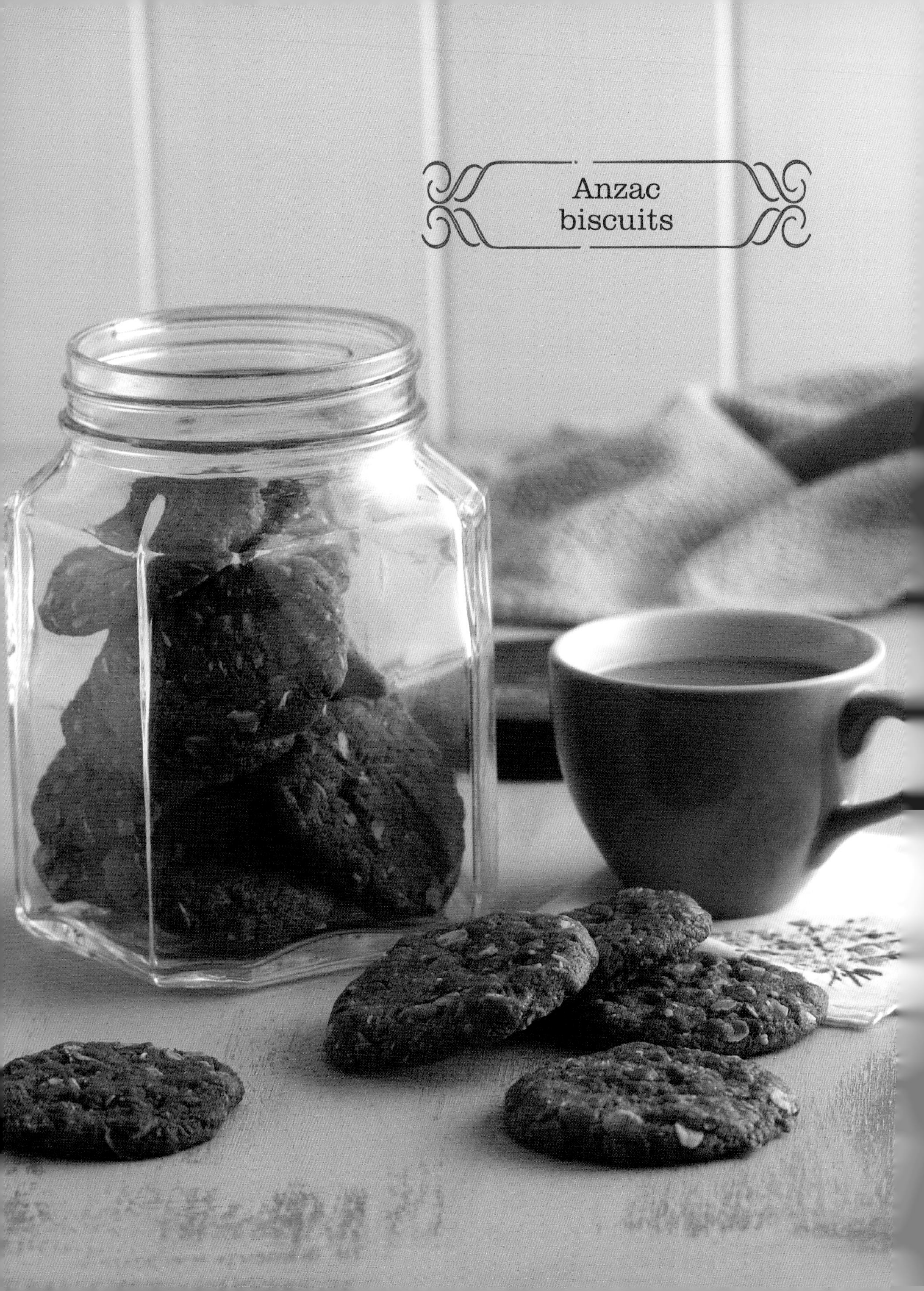

Anzac biscuits

Rita Beattie, Crookwell Show

Ingredients

1 cup plain flour
1 cup rolled oats
1 cup sugar
¾ cup coconut
115g (4 oz) butter
2 tablespoons golden syrup
1 teaspoon bicarbonate soda

Method

Preheat oven to 170ºC (330ºF), fan high. Grease an oven, baking or slide tray. In a bowl combine the flour, oats, sugar and coconut. Put the butter and golden syrup in a saucepan and heat until butter is melted. Add bicarbonate soda mixed with 2 tablespoons boiling water to syrup mixture, stir and pour into dry ingredients. Mix well. Place a teaspoon of mixture on tray and flatten with a fork. Cook for 20 minutes or until golden brown. Leave biscuits on tray to cool slightly before removing onto cake cooler.

Chocolate chip biscuits

Diane Blanch, Kangaroo Valley Show

Ingredients

125g (4 oz) butter
½ cup castor sugar
½ cup brown sugar
1 teaspoon vanilla essence
1 egg
2 cups self-raising flour
1 cup chocolate chips

Method

Preheat oven to 180°C (350°F).
Grease a baking tray.
In a bowl place butter, castor sugar, brown sugar and vanilla essence. Beat until light and creamy. Add egg and beat until combined. Add the flour and chocolate chips and combine to a soft dough.
Roll tablespoon portions of dough into a ball and flatten. Place evenly on tray.
Bake in oven for 12–15 minutes.

. . . .

Coconut and lemon biscuits

Margaret Weeks, Cooma Show

Pastry

Ingredients

90g (3 oz) butter
¼ cup sugar
½ teaspoon vanilla
1 cup plain flour
1 eggwhite

Method

Preheat oven to 180ºC (350ºF).
Beat butter, sugar and vanilla until creamy.
Add flour, mix well to form a ball. Place on
floured board, roll out to 3mm thickness.
Cut out 5cm (2 in) rounds. Using a 2.5cm
(1 in) cutter, cut the centres out of half the
pastry rounds, these will be the tops. Place
bases and tops on baking paper on a tray,
brush these with eggwhite and sprinkle with
coconut. Bake in oven for
10 minutes, or until lightly browned. When
cool, spread a teaspoonful of the lemon
filling on the biscuit base then place coconut
covered tops over the filling.

Lemon filling

Ingredients

1½ tablespoons sugar
2 tablespoons cornflour
2 tablespoons lemon juice
¾ cup water
1 egg yolk
45g (1½ oz) butter

Method

Place sugar and cornflour in saucepan,
add lemon juice and blend to a smooth paste.
Stir in water, add egg yolk and butter and
continue stirring until mixture boils
and thickens.
Cool before placing on biscuit.

Makes 20 biscuits

· ·

Coconut jam biscuits

Tony Griffin, Junee Show

Ingredients

125g (4 oz) butter
½ cup sugar
1 egg, well beaten
¼ cup desiccated coconut
2 cups plain flour
1 teaspoon baking powder
2 tablespoons raspberry or strawberry jam

Method

Preheat oven to 160°C (320°F).
Grease a baking tray.
Cream butter and sugar together. Add egg and mix well. Add coconut, sifted flour and baking powder. Roll mixture into small balls and place on greased baking tray. Make a small well in centre of each ball and place a small teaspoon of jam in well. Bake for approximately 15 minutes or until firm to touch. Place on cake rack to cool.

Makes 12–15

. . . .

Coconut cookies

Phil Fisher, Kiama Show

Ingredients

¼ cup butter
¾ cup brown sugar
1 cup coconut
1 cup self-raising flour

Method

Preheat oven to 180° (350°F).
Cream butter and sugar together.
Add coconut and flour and combine.
Press mixture into a flat dish or slice tin and bake for about 20 minutes. Cut while hot and ice with lemon icing.

Lemon icing

Ingredients

2 cups icing sugar
2 tablespoons butter, soft
juice of 1 lemon

Method

Combine sugar and butter in a bowl and blend. Add lemon juice to blend and cream thoroughly until smooth.

Makes 20 biscuits

Ginger biscuits

Ruth Chittick, Bowral Show

Ingredients

225g (8 oz) shortening
(½ butter, ½ margarine)
225g (8 oz) brown sugar
225g (8 oz) plain flour
1 egg
½ teaspoon vanilla
2 tablespoons cornflour
3 teaspoons ginger
1 teaspoon cinnamon
1 teaspoon allspice
½ cup sultanas (optional)

Method

Preheat oven to 160°C (325°F).
Grease well a biscuit tray.
In a large bowl, beat shortening and sugar
to a cream. Add egg and vanilla.
Sift dry ingredients together and add to
mixture. Spread onto a greased biscuit tray.
Mark into slices or fingers and bake in oven
for 10–15 minutes. Cool in tin, turn out and
complete cutting.

Makes about 24 biscuits

Gingernut biscuits

Joyce Orgill, Cootamundra Show

I have been a stewardess in the cooking section for over 35 years and have enjoyed being a competitor and the friendships I have made during this time. My advice to all would-be competitors, is to read the schedule twice and observe the rules to avoid disqualification.

Ingredients

125g (4 oz) softened margarine/butter
180g (6 oz) sugar
1 egg
2 tablespoons golden syrup
250g (8 oz) plain flour
1 teaspoon bicarbonate soda
1 dessertspoon ground ginger

Method

Preheat oven to 180°C (350°F).
Grease a baking tray.
Cream butter and sugar together.
Add egg and golden syrup.
Sift flour, soda and ginger together. Add to butter mixture and mix well. Drop small spoonfuls onto baking tray and bake in oven for 10 minutes.

· ·

Delicious sticky gingerbread

Sarah Wray, Penrith Show

Ingredients

180g (6 oz) butter, cut into small pieces
1 cup water
1 cup golden syrup
2 eggs, well beaten
360g (12 oz) plain flour
2 teaspoons baking soda
2 teaspoons mixed spice
2 teaspoons cinnamon
3 teaspoons ground ginger
250g (8 oz) brown sugar

Method

Preheat oven to 180°C (350°F).
Grease a 20cm (8 in) square tin.
Warm the butter with the water and golden syrup, just enough to melt the butter. Remove from heat.
In a large bowl sift together the flour, soda, spices and sugar. Pour the beaten eggs and liquid ingredients into the sifted ingredients and mix well. The mixture will seem very wet.
Pour into the tin. Bake for 1–1½ hours.
Allow the gingerbread to cool for a while in the tin before turning out.

Note: Keeps extremely well for several days in airtight container.

· ·

Ginger gems

Heather Younger, Lithgow Show

This recipe works best using a gem iron, a cast-iron baking tin divided into small curved spaces.

Ingredients

125g (4 oz) butter
½ cup sugar
2 eggs
4 level tablespoons golden syrup
4 level teaspoons ground ginger
pinch of salt
2 cups plain flour
2 level teaspoons bicarbonate soda
$^2/_3$ cup milk

Method

Preheat oven to 190°C (375°F).
Grease well a gem iron.
Cream butter and sugar until light. Add eggs.
Mix in golden syrup. Dissolve bicarbonate
soda in milk. Sift dry ingredients and add
to creamed mixture alternately with milk
mixture. Bake in heated gem iron in oven for
8–10 minutes. Cool, split in half and spread
with butter.

Makes 12

Old fashioned gingerbread

Esme McRae, Armidale and New England Show

Ingredients

125g (4 oz) butter
½ cup treacle
¼ cup golden syrup
½ cup milk
2 eggs
2 cups plain flour
1 teaspoon spice
1 tablespoon ground ginger
1 teaspoon baking soda
salt
crystallised ginger, to decorate

Method

Preheat oven to 150°C (300°F). Grease a 20cm (8 in) tin.
In a saucepan place butter, treacle, golden syrup and milk and heat gently on the stove until butter melts. Let cool. Beat eggs and add to cooled mixture.
Add flour, salt, baking soda, spice and ground ginger and mix further.
Pour in mixture and cook for 1 hour.
When cold, ice with lemon icing and decorate with crystallised ginger.

Lemon icing

Ingredients

2 cups icing sugar
2 tablespoons butter, soft
juice of 1 lemon

Method

Combine sugar and butter in a bowl and blend. Add lemon juice to blend and cream thoroughly until smooth.

. . . .

Jam drops

Leanne Sinclair, Dorrigo Show

Ingredients

½ cup butter
¾ cup sugar
2 eggs
2 cups plain flour
2 teaspoons baking powder
2 tablespoons raspberry or strawberry jam

Method

Preheat oven to 200°C (400°F).
Beat butter and sugar to a cream.
Add eggs and then sifted flour and baking
powder. Make into small stiff balls and press
a hole in the centre and fill with a small
teaspoon of jam. Bake in oven for
10–15 minutes or until brown.

· ·

Powder puffs

Gwen Fairman, Ariah Park Show

Ingredients

3 eggs, separated
¾ cup sugar
¾ cup plain flour
½ cup cornflour
1 teaspoon baking powder

Method

Preheat oven to 230°C (450°F).
Grease well an oven slide or baking tray.
In a bowl, beat eggwhites and sugar until stiff.
Add egg yolks and beat 7 minutes in
a mixmaster. Sift flour, cornflour and
baking powder together and fold in. Drop
dessertspoon of mixture onto tray and cook
in oven for approximately 5 mintues, or until
light brown.

Note: Greaseproof paper along the sides will
stop the puffs from hardening on the edge.

Shortbread rounds

June Mason, Finley Show

Ingredients

225g (½ lb) butter
115g (4 oz) castor sugar
1½ cups plain flour
¼ teaspoon salt

Method

Preheat oven to 180ºC (350ºF).
Rub butter into dry ingredients to make dough. Make into individual biscuits or two rounds 15cm (6 in) round and 0.5cm (¼ in) thick and and cut into 8 pieces.
Bake in oven for approximately 35–40 minutes.

Tip

Don't overcook shortbread, it contains no eggs so the dough requires very little baking. Cook until just tinged with gold at the edges.

· ·

Shortbread

Val Davidson, Mungindi Show

Ingredients

100g (3½ oz) butter
¼ cup castor sugar
1¼–1½ cups plain flour

Method

Preheat oven to 150°C (300°F).
Cream butter and sugar together until white.
Add sifted flour to form a stiff dough. Turn
out on floured board, knead and divide into
two pieces. Place on bottom of an upturned
sponge tin. Press each into circles of
approximately 2cm (¾ in) thickness and pinch
edges. Mark into sections and prick well.
Bake in oven for approximately 45 minutes.

Shortbread

Macadamia shortbread

Mervene McIntosh, Griffith Show

Mervene McIntosh started exhibiting at the Griffith Show in 2001. Since that first year of exhibiting Mervene has won many 1st, 2nds, Most Successful's, and Champion Exhibit Prizes. The following recipe is one of Mervene's favourites, which she has one 1st prize with a number of times.

Ingredients

250g (8 oz) butter chopped
½ cup castor sugar
2 teaspoons vanilla essence
2 cups plain flour
½ cup rice flour or ground rice
½ cup finely chopped macadamias
2 tablespoons sugar, extra

Method

Preheat oven to 160°C (325°F).
Lightly grease an oven tray.
Beat butter, sugar and vanilla in small bowl with electric mixer until pale and fluffy. Transfer mixture to large bowl, stir in sifted flours and nuts in two batches.
Press ingredients together. Knead on a lightly floured surface until smooth (do not over knead). Divide into two portions. Roll each portion between two sheets of baking paper to form a a 23cm (9 in) circle. Press an upturned 22cm (8½ in) loose-based fluted flan tin into shortbread to cut rounds.
Cut each round into 16 wedges. Place on trays; mark the biscuit wedges with a fork and sprinkle with extra sugar.
Bake in oven for about 20 minutes or until a pale straw colour. Stand for 10 minutes before transferring to a rack to cool.

Note: suitable to freeze.

Makes 32

· ·

Crunchie biscuits

Esme McRae, Armidale and New England Show

Ingredients

½ cup of butter
1 tablespoon golden syrup
1 teaspoon bicarbonate soda
1¼ cups self-raising flour
1 cup sugar
1 cup coconut
1 cup rolled oats
salt

Method

Preheat oven to 180°C (350°F).
Grease an oven tray.
In a saucepan melt butter with golden syrup.
Dissolve bicarbonate soda in 2 tablespoons of
boiling water and add to the saucepan.
Mix in the rest of the ingredients.
Drop in teaspoonfuls on tray.
Bake in oven for 6–10 minutes, or until
golden brown. The longer you bake them the
crunchier the biscuits.

Apricot, date
& walnut slice

· ·

Apricot, date & walnut slice

Helen Mohr, Weethalle Show

Ingredients

1 cup chopped apricots, soaked for an hour
1 cup of sugar
½ cup chopped dates
½ cup chopped walnuts
2 cups self-raising flour
170g (6 oz) butter or margarine, melted

Method

Preheat oven to 180°C (350°F).
Place all the dry ingredients in a large bowl.
Add the melted butter and combine.
Press into a lamington tin and bake in oven
for 20 minutes.

. . . .

Apricot yoghurt slice

May Harris, Nambucca River Show

Ingredients

125g (4 oz) unsalted butter,
room temperature
1 cup castor sugar
2 eggs
2 teaspoons finely grated lemon rind
1½ cups self-raising flour
1$^{1}/_{3}$ cups plain yoghurt
1 x 250g packet soft and juicy apricots,
finely chopped
cinnamon sugar, to decorate

Method

Preheat oven to 180°C (350°F).
Grease an 18cm x 28cm (7 in x 11 in)
rectangular slice pan and line the base and
long sides with baking paper.
Place butter, sugar, eggs, lemon rind, flour
and yoghurt in the small bowl of an electric
mixer. Beat on low speed until just combined.
Increase speed to medium and beat for about
3 minutes or until mixture is smooth and
changed in colour. Stir in apricots.
Pour into slice pan and cook in oven for about
45 minutes, or until cooked when tested.
When cooked, remove from oven and stand
in pan for 5 minutes before turning on a wire
rack to cool. Spread icing over slice, cut into
slices and dust with cinnamon sugar.

Cream cheese frosting

Ingredients

50g (2 oz) cream cheese at room temperature
24g (1 oz) unsalted butter at room
temperature
1½ cups icing sugar mixture

Method

Beat cream cheese and butter in the small
bowl of an electric mixer until light and
creamy. Add icing sugar mixture in two
batches. Beat until smooth.

Makes 10

Cream slice

Margaret Barron, Cooma Show

Base

Ingredients

½ cup sugar
1 beaten egg
185g (6 oz) butter or margarine, melted
1 ½ cups self-raising flour

Method

Preheat oven to 180ºC (350ºF).
Grease a 23cm x 30cm (9 in x 12 in) slab tin.
Mix sugar and egg together. Add melted
butter and egg mixture to flour and mix to
combine. Press into tin and cook in oven for
10–15 minutes until golden and cooked.
Let cool.

First filling

Ingredients

1 x 395g tin condensed milk
1 tin reduced cream
½ cup lemon juice

Method

Beat ingredients together until thick. Spread
over cooled base and leave to set.

Second filling

Ingredients

1½ cups water
1 cup sugar
2 tablespoons custard powder
pulp of 2 passionfruit (optional)

Method

Place all ingredients into a saucepan and boil,
stirring constantly, until thick. When nearly
cooled, spread over cream filling and chill.

. . . .

Choc chip apricot slice

Heather Starr, Guyra Show

Ingredients

1 cup chopped dried apricots
1 cup apricot nectar
125g (4 oz) butter
$^2/_3$ cup raw sugar
2 eggs
1½ cups coconut
1½ cups self-raising flour
½ cup choc bits
icing sugar, to serve (optional)

Method

Preheat oven to 180ºC (350ºF).
Grease a deep slice tin.
Combine apricots and nectar in a saucepan
and heat, do not boil, then allow to cool.
Cream butter and sugar together. Add eggs
and transfer mixture to large bowl. Stir
in coconut then half the sifted flour. Add
apricots and nectar then the rest of the flour
and choc bits. Bake in tin in oven for 25–30
minutes. If desired, dust with sifted icing
sugar to serve.

Black forest slice

....

Black forest slice

Kevin Baldwin, Newcastle Regional Show

Ingredients

125g (4 oz) butter
¾ cup brown sugar
1 egg, beaten
1 tablespoon golden syrup
½ cup desiccated coconut
1 cup self-raising flour
2 dessertspoons cocoa
2 tablespoons milk
½ teaspoon vanilla essence

Method

Preheat oven to 180°C (350°F).
Grease and line a 29cm x 18cm (12 in x 7 in) lamington tin.
Melt butter and beat in brown sugar. Add egg and golden syrup and mix well. Add coconut, flour and cocoa. Stir in milk and vanilla essence. Spread into lamington tin and bake for 20 minutes. Allow to cool. Spread on topping, arrange cherries on top and sprinkle all over with chocolate sprinkles. Cut in squares to serve

Topping

Ingredients

300ml (10 fl oz) cream
1 tablespoon icing sugar
3 tablespoons port
1 x 440g can pitted black cherries, well drained
chocolate sprinkles

Method

Whip cream, then stir in icing sugar and port and mix well.

. . . .

Caramel chocolate slice

Betty Eade, Wingham Show

Ingredients

1 cup self-raising flour
1 cup coconut
1 cup brown sugar, firmly packed
125g (4 oz) butter, melted

Method

Preheat oven to 180°C (350°F).
Lightly grease a slice tin. Combine sifted flour, coconut, brown sugar and melted butter and stir to combine.
Press mixture over base of prepared tin and bake in oven for 15 minutes. Pour hot filling over base and return to oven for 10 minutes. Cool. Spread warm topping over filling and let stand at room temperature until set—about 2–3 hours.

Filling

Ingredients

1 x 400g tin condensed milk
30g (1 oz) butter
2 tablespoons golden syrup

Method

Combine condensed milk, butter and golden syrup in a pan over low heat until butter is melted.

Topping

Ingredients

125g (4 oz) dark chocolate chopped
30g (1 oz) butter

Method

Combine chocolate and butter in a pan over low heat until smooth.

. . . .

Kit Kat slice

Kevin Baldwin, Newcastle Regional Show

Ingredients

3 x 90g Kit Kat bars, crushed
50g (2 oz) butter, melted

Method

Combine crushed Kit Kat bars and melted butter. Press into base of a greased and lined 18cm x 28cm (7 in x 11 in) lamington tin. Chill in the refrigerator for 1 hour.

Topping

Ingredients

375g (12 oz) cream cheese
½ cup castor sugar
2 eggs
300ml (10 fl oz) sour cream
1 teaspoon vanilla
100g (3½ oz) choc melts
2 tablespoons black coffee

Method

Preheat oven to 180°C (350°F).
Beat cream cheese and sugar together until light. Add eggs, one at a time, and mix well. Fold in sour cream and vanilla. Pour over prepared base. Melt choc melts and coffee together. Mix well and drizzle over topping. Bake in oven for 35–40 minutes. When cooked, remove from oven and cool on a wire rack. Cut into squares to serve.

. . . .

Cheesecake slice

Kevin Baldwin, Newcastle Regional Show

Ingredients

250g (8 oz) Granita biscuits, crushed
½ cup desiccated coconut
150g (5 oz) butter, melted
250g (8 oz) cream cheese, softened to room temperature
½ cup sour cream
½ cup castor sugar
2 eggs, separated
1 tablespoon lemon juice
2 teaspoons plain flour
½ cup jam (blueberry, raspberry, strawberry or blackberry)

Method

Preheat oven to 160°C (315°F).
Line and lightly grease 18cm x 28cm (7 in x 11 in) shallow tin with baking paper.
In a bowl add crushed biscuits, coconut and melted butter and mix until well combined.
Press firmly into the tin and chill.
Beat cream cheese, sour cream and sugar until smooth. Add egg yolks, lemon juice and flour and mix well. Set aside.
Spread the jam over the chilled base.
Beat the eggwhite into stiff peaks and fold into the cream cheese mixture.
Pour over the base and smooth. Bake for 45–55 minutes, or until golden brown.
Cool in the tin then remove and slice into squares or diamonds.

. . . .

Fruit slice

Tony Griffin, Junee Show

Soak the fruit for this slice overnight.

Ingredients

1 cup of mixed fruit (raisins or dates)
1 tablespoon sherry
115g (¼ lb) shortening
1 cup of brown sugar
1 egg
1½ cups self-raising flour
1½ teaspoons cinnamon

Method

Preheat oven to 200°C (400°F).
Grease a Swiss roll tin.
Soak mixed fruit in some sweet sherry or port overnight before making slice.
Melt shortening and mix with sugar.
Add egg and beat well. Add the soaked fruit.
Lastly add flour and cinnamon. Bake in oven for 20–25 minutes. When cold cut into fingers or slices.

Passionfruit slice

Phil Fisher, Kiama Show

Ingredients

1 cup self-raising flour
1 cup coconut
½ cup white sugar
113g (¼ lb) butter, melted
1 teaspoon vanilla
cream, to serve

Method

Preheat oven to 180°C (350°F).
Mix dry ingredients together. Add melted
butter and vanilla. Put in slice tin and bake in
oven for 15 minutes. Allow to cool.
Reduce oven temperature to 150°C (300°F).
Spread on topping and bake in oven for
10 minutes. Allow to cool and spread
with cream.

Topping

Ingredients

1 x 395ml tin condensed milk
juice of 2 lemons
2 passionfruit

Method

Mix together condensed milk, lemon juice
and passionfruit.

....

Rennies slice

Margaret Barron, Cooma Show

Ingredients

1 cup self-raising flour
1 cup coconut
1 cup rolled oats
1 cup castor sugar
115g (4 ozs) butter
1 teaspoon honey
1 egg beaten

Method

Preheat oven to 150°C (300°F). Grease a 23cm x 30cm (9 in x 12 in) slice tin. Combine flour, coconut, rolled oats and sugar into a bowl. Melt butter and honey. Add to dry ingredients with egg. Mix well and press into slice tin. You can press extra oats onto the top. Cook in oven until golden and cooked—15–20 minutes, be careful, it burns easily.

Cooked
Coconut slice

. . . .

Cooked coconut slice

Tottie Pownall OAM, Narrabri Show

Tottie was involved with the show society for about 40 years as a cooking steward, head steward and judge. She stopped competing in 2000 when she moved into the aged care hostel and no longer had a kitchen but she has continued to do some judging. Tottie's younger daughter, Narrabri's first female president, and oldest son were presidents of the show society as well.

Ingredients

2 cups sugar
½ cup milk
1 dessertspoon arrowroot
¾ cup coconut
pinch cream of tartar
flavouring and/or colour such as cochineal
(optional)

Method

Boil together sugar, milk and arrowroot for 5 minutes. Add coconut and boil for a further minute. Make sure sugar is dissolved before mixture boils. Brush down any crystals that form on the side of the pan. Add flavouring and/or colour and cream of tartar and beat using an electric beater until thick. Set in a 15cm (6 in) biscuit tray or cake tin.
In summer you may need to put the basin in cold water for it to thicken. In winter you may have to be quick.

Note: If you want two-coloured coconut ice, double this quantity to make 2 separate batches and use a 20cm (8 in) tin. Colour one batch pink with cochineal and scoop on top of the white layer.

Tip

When making coconut ice, make sure the sugar is dissolved before the mixture boils. Brush down any crystals that form on the side of the pan.

. . . .

Coconut raspberry slice

Robyn Blackstock, Parkes Show

Ingredients

90g (3 oz) butter
½ cup castor sugar
1 egg
$^1/_3$ cup self-raising flour
$^2/_3$ cup plain flour
½ cup raspberry jam

Method

Preheat oven to 180°C (350°F). Grease a Swiss roll tin. Cream butter, sugar and eggs together. Stir in flour and press evenly into tin. Bake in oven for 10 minutes. Remove from oven and spread with jam, then topping. Bake in oven for a further 35 minutes.

Topping

Ingredients

2 eggs
$^1/_3$ cup castor sugar
2 cups coconut

Method

Beat eggs lightly. Mix in sugar and coconut.

Coconut
raspberry slice

Pecan caramel slice

Una Greco, Picton Show

Ingredients

125g (4 oz) butter
¼ cup castor sugar
1 cup plain flour
¼ cup self-raising flour
1 cup chopped pecans

Method

Preheat oven to 180°C (350°F). Grease a 19cm x 29cm (7½ in x 11 in) lamington pan. Combine butter and sugar in a small bowl and beat with electric mixer until light and fluffy. Stir in sifted flours. Press dough evenly over base of prepared pan and bake in oven for about 12 minutes or until firm. Cool for 10 minutes. Spread filling over the base, sprinkle with nuts, bake in oven for about 10 minutes, or until golden brown. Let slice cool in pan before cutting.

Filling

Ingredients

1 x 400g tin sweetened condensed milk
30g (1 oz) butter
2 tablespoons golden syrup

Method

Combine all ingredients in a small saucepan. Stir over low heat (or microwave on high for about a minute) until mixture is heated through.

Pecan crunchies

Elaine Warren, Boorowa Show

Ingredients

125g (4 oz) butter
$^2/_3$ cup raw sugar
2 tablespoons golden syrup
1 egg
1 cup coconut
1½ cups wholemeal self-raising flour
pecan kernels, to decorate

Method

Preheat oven to 125°C (250°F).
Grease a biscuit tray.
Melt butter in a saucepan. Add sugar, golden syrup and egg and stir until combined.
Stir in coconut and flour. Roll teaspoonfuls of mixture into balls between floured hands and place on biscuit tray and press a pecan on top of each biscuit and flatten slightly.
Bake for 30–35 minutes.

Makes 18–20

· ·

Licorice allsort slice

Robyn Blackstock, Parkes Show

Ingredients

250g (8 oz) crushed Marie biscuits
½ cup coconut
550g (1 lb) licorice allsorts, chopped
125g (4 oz) margarine
1 tablespoon golden syrup
300g (10 oz) condensed milk

Method

Mix crushed biscuit, coconut and licorice allsorts together. In a saucepan add margarine, golden syrup and condensed milk. Pour onto biscuit mixture and mix to combine. Press into a large greased slice tin 20cm x 30cm (8 in x 12 in). Pour topping over base and let set in fridge for 15 minutes before cutting into small squares.

Topping

Ingredients

10g ($^1/_3$ oz) copha
200g (7 oz) milk chocolate, melted

Method

Combine ingredients in a saucepan on the stove on low heat until melted.

Makes 24

. . . .

Rum & raisin slice

Margaret Bilbow, Parkes Show

Ingredients

½ cup raisins
⅓ cup dark rum
200g (1 oz) dark chocolate,
chopped into small, even-sized pieces
60g (2 oz) unsalted butter,
chopped into small, even-sized pieces
½ cup castor sugar
1 cup thick cream
1 cup plain flour
3 eggs, lightly beaten
cocoa powder, to dust

Method

Preheat the oven to 180°C (350°F). Lightly grease an 18cm x 28cm (7 in x 11 in) shallow baking tin and line with baking paper, leaving it to hang over on two opposite sides. Combine the raisins and rum. Place the chocolate and butter in a heatproof bowl. Bring a saucepan of water to the boil and remove from the heat. Sit the heatproof bowl over the pan, ensuring the bowl doesn't touch the water and allow to stand, stirring occasionally, until melted. Stir in the castor sugar and cream. Sift the flour into another bowl. Add the raisins, chocolate mixture and eggs and mix well. Pour into the tin and smooth the surface. Bake for 25–30 minutes, or until just set. Cool completely then refrigerate overnight. Cut into small pieces and sprinkle liberally with cocoa powder.

. . . .

Date slice

Anny Kelly, Mungindi Show

Biscuit base

Ingredients

90g (3 oz) butter
1½ cups self-raising flour
pinch salt
1 tablespoon brown sugar
¼ cup water

Method

Rub butter into flour and salt. Add sugar and mix to a firm dough with water. Press into swiss roll tin. Spread over date filling. Bake in oven for 35–40 minutes. Allow to cool in tin. Ice if desired and sprinkle with cinnamon.

Date filling

Ingredients

225g (½ lb) dates
½ cup brown sugar
½ teaspoon spice
½ cup water
1 dessertspoon lemon juice

Method

Place all ingredients in saucepan, cook over gentle heat until thick. Let cool.

Icing

Ingredients

90g (3 oz) butter
½ cup brown sugar
1 egg
1 cup self-raising flour
½ cup milk
cinnamon, optional

Method

Preheat oven to 180°C (350°F). Cream butter with brown sugar. Add egg. Fold in flour alternatively with milk and combine well.

189

Macadamia shortcake slice

May Harris, Nambucca River Show

Ingredients

250g (8 oz) butter,
softened to room temperature
¾ cup castor sugar
4 x 60g eggs
2 cups self-raising flour, sifted
200g (7 oz) macadamia halves
6 tablespoons warmed apricot conserve
1 tablespoon extra castor sugar

Method

Preheat oven to 180°C (350°F).
Grease a 30cm x 20cm x 4cm deep
(12 in x 8 in x 1½ in) pan with baking paper.
Beat butter and sugar together in a bowl until
thick and creamy, about 5 minutes.
Beat in eggs, beating well after each addition.
Stir in flour and half the macadamias well, to
make quite a stiff mixture.
Using a spatula, spread half the cake
mixture over the pan base and spoon over
the warm conserve. Spread over remaining
cake mixture to reach pan sides. Press in
remaining macadamias and sprinkle with
extra sugar. Bake for 25–30 minutes or until a
skewer inserted comes out clean. Cover with
baking paper if browning too much.
Remove from oven and stand 5 minutes
before turning out onto a rack to cool.
Cut into 5cm (2 in) squares.

. . . .

Passion mallow slice

Kae Anforth, Bellinger Show

Ingredients

150g (5 oz) butter, softened
¼ cup castor sugar
½ teaspoon vanilla essence
1 cup plain flour
½ cup self-raising flour

Method

Preheat oven to 180°C (350°F) or
160°C (325°F) fan-forced).
Lightly grease an 18cm x 28cm (7 in x 11 in)
slice pan and line with baking paper.
Beat butter, sugar and vanilla essence in a
small bowl with electric mixer until creamy.
Sift flour together and stir into creamed
mixture. Press mixture into prepared pan,
prick all over with fork and bake for about
25 minutes, or until golden brown.

Marshmallow topping

Ingredients

½ cup passionfruit pulp
250g (8 oz) white marshmallows
½ cup milk
2 tablespoons castor sugar
2 teaspoons lemon juice
1¼ cups thickened cream, whipped lightly

Method

Put passionfruit, marshmallows, milk and
sugar in a saucepan and stir over low heat
until marshmallows are melted. Stir in lemon
juice and transfer to a bowl. Refrigerate,
stirring occasionally, until thickened
slightly—approximately 30 minutes.
Fold in whipped cream. To serve, pour
topping over base then refrigerate until set.
Cut into pieces. Top with moist coconut flakes
if desired.

Note: This recipe is not suitable for freezing.

Peanut caramel bars

Joy Schultz, The Rock Show

Ingredients

125g (4 oz) butter
½ cup sugar
1 egg yolk
¼ cup self-raising flour
1 cup plain flour
2 tablespoons custard powder
¼ teaspoon salt

Method

Preheat oven to 180°C (350°F).
Grease a lamington tin.
Cream butter and sugar until light and fluffy.
Add egg yolk and mix well. Add sifted flours,
custard powder and salt. Mix to a firm dough.
Press mixture into base of lamington tin
and bake in oven for 15 minutes, or until
golden brown. Remove from oven. Spread
with topping. Return to moderate oven for a
further 5 minutes. Allow to cool in tin then cut
into squares.

Topping

Ingredients

½ cup brown sugar, lightly packed
1 tablespoon golden syrup
90g (3 oz) butter
125g (4 oz) roasted peanuts, unsalted,
roughly chopped

Method

Place brown sugar, golden syrup and butter
in small saucepan. Stir over low heat until
butter is melted and sugar is dissolved.
Simmer gently for 5 minutes. Stir in nuts.

Pickles, chutneys & relishes

. . . .

Choko pickles

Dulcie Martin, Morisset Show

Ingredients

1.8kg (4 lb) chokos
907g (2 lb) onions
450g (1 lb) cauliflower
950ml (2 pints) vinegar
675g (1½ lb) brown sugar
1 cup plain flour
1 tablespoons mustard
1 tablespoon turmeric
2 dessertspoons curry powder

Method

Boil vegetables until tender and drain.
Put vinegar and sugar in saucepan and bring
to boil. Add vegetables and bring back to boil.
Blend flour and spices with a dash of vinegar.
Mix to make a thick paste. Add to saucepan,
stirring all the time. Bottle while hot.

Makes about 10 medium-sized jars

Tip

It's best to use plastic lids rather than metal lids on jars
when bottling. Metal lids can react with the salt and vinegars
used in the recipe.

. . . .

Mustard pickles

Patricia Williams, Baradine Show

Ingredients

1kg (2 lb) green tomatoes, chopped
1½kg (3 lb) cauliflower, chopped
3 large onions, chopped
2 large green apples, chopped
1 small cup salt
3 tablespoons mustard
4 large cups sugar
1 tablespoon turmeric
2 teaspoons curry powder
½ teaspoon pepper
2 large tablespoons plain flour
400ml (13 fl oz) white vinegar

Method

Place the tomatoes, cauliflower, onions and apples in a saucepan. Add salt, cover with water and let stand overnight.
The next day, cook on the stovetop until vegetables are tender and then drain.
Place in a basin the mustard, sugar, turmeric, curry powder, pepper and flour. Add a small amount of vinegar and mix to make a smooth paste. Add the remaining vinegar and pour mixture into the drained vegetables. Cook over medium heat for 10 minutes, stirring to prevent burning. Bottle while hot.

Green tomato
pickles

Green tomato pickles

Cassandra Goodworth, Bellinger River Show

Ingredients

1.8kg (4 lb) green tomatoes, quartered
0.8kg (2 lb) onions, quartered
¼ cup salt
0.8kg (2 lb) brown sugar
750ml vinegar
2 tablespoons mustard
1 tablespoon curry
1 dessertspoon turmeric
½ cup plain flour

Method

Place tomato and onion in a saucepan, cover with warm water and salt and leave overnight. Next morning cook for half an hour then strain off the juices. Add sugar and vinegar and cook again until sugar is melted and ingredients are combined. Thicken with remaining ingredients. Bottle in warm jars and seal.

. . . .

Mixed clear pickles

Eveyln Strong, Berry Show

You can use other vegetables of your choice for this recipe.

Ingredients

2 cups water
1 cup white vinegar
½ cup white sugar
1 green tomato, quartered
3 green beans
1 stalk of celery
1 small cucumber
½ red capsicum
½ green capsicum
2 pieces of cauliflower
carrot sticks
few peppercorns

Method

In a saucepan, boil water, vinegar and sugar until sugar has dissolved.
Blanch vegetables in saucepan in batches, add peppercorns and bottle. Pour hot vinegar mixture evenly into bottles and seal.

Tip

You should always sterilise jars before you bottle.
Wash jars and lids thoroughly in hot, soapy water.
Rinse in hot water, then place in a hot oven for 10–15 minutes.
It's a good idea to do this while you are preparing the jam.

· ·

Pickled zucchini

Debbie Allan, Griffith Show

As well as competing successfully in foodstuffs at the show, Debbie has also won the Nell Davidge Most Successful Pavilion Exhibitor on several occasions, which also encompasses photography, fine arts, knitting, crochet, horticulture, produce and fruit & vegetables. Most of the produce in her preserves comes from her own garden. This recipe is handed down from her grandmother.

Ingredients

1kg (2 lb) zucchini, finely chopped
2 large onions, finely sliced
2 teaspoons salt

Method

Place the zucchini and onion in an ice-cream container, sprinkle with salt, stir slightly and let stand 2 hours.

Brine

Ingredients

1½ cups sugar
1½ cups white vinegar
¾ teaspoon turmeric
1 teaspoon celery seeds
2 teaspoons mustard seeds
2–3 shakes pepper

Method

Place brine ingredients in a saucepan, bring to the boil and simmer 5 minutes.
Place vegetables in an ice-cream container and fill to the brim with cold water. Stir, then tip contents into a colander to drain well.
Place the drained vegetables into the boiling brine and stir well. Remove from heat and let stand for 2 hours. Bring back to boil, simmer for 5 minutes. Spoon into jars and seal.

Makes 8–10 jars

. . . .

Spicy mustard pickles

Vicki Lawrence, Dorrigo Show

Ingredients

¼ medium cauliflower,
chopped into even pieces
250g (8 oz) green beans,
chopped into even pieces
3 medium onions, chopped into even pieces
1 medium red capsicum
¼ cup coarse cooking salt
2 tablespoons seeded mustard
2 teaspoons curry powder
¼ teaspoon turmeric
1¾ cup white vinegar plus a little extra
1 cup brown sugar, firmly packed
2 tablespoons plain flour
¼ cup extra white vinegar

Method

Combine cauliflower, beans, onions and
capsicum in a large bowl, sprinkle with the
salt and let sit overnight.
The next day, rinse in a colander under
running cold water and drain.
Combine vegetables, mustards, curry powder,
turmeric, vinegar and sugar in a large frypan
and stir over heat until sugar has dissolved.
Bring to the boil for about 10 minutes or
until vegetables are tender. Blend the flour
with the extra vinegar and stir in. Continue
cooking over heat until mixture thickens.
Pour into hot sterilised jars and seal.

Sweet mustard pickles

Frances Charlton, Parkes Show

Frances has been competing at the Parkes Show for over 60 years and has won many prizes and ribbons. Her first success was for a sponge sandwich in the under-14 section, but this recipe is for her tasty pickles.

Ingredients

1.5kg (3 lb) green tomatoes, chokos, or a mixture of vegetables, chopped
3 large onions, chopped
1 tablespoon salt
1.75 litres (60 fl oz) white vinegar
1kg (2 lb) white sugar
3 tablespoons mustard
1 tablespoon turmeric
1 cup plain flour

Method

Place the vegetables in a pot and sprinkle with salt. Leave for half a day or overnight. The next day, boil the vegetables in a pot until just tender. Strain off the brine.
Put vegetables back on the stove, add most of the vinegar and all the sugar. Bring back to the boil and thicken with the dry ingredients mixed with the rest of vinegar and a little water if needed. Keep stirring for a further 5 minutes. Take off the heat and let stand for 10 minutes. Bottle and seal.

· ·

Vegetable pickles

Ros Edwards, Parkes Show

Ingredients

1.5kg (3 lb) vegetables
(any one vegetable or a variety of
vegetables can be used e.g. melon, chokos,
cucumbers, cauliflower, beans, green or ripe
tomatoes, onions)
1½ cups sugar
2 cups vinegar
1 level tablespoon salt
1 tablespoon mustard
1 tablespoon curry
1 dessertspoon of turmeric
½ cup cornflour or plain flour

Method

Boil vegetables, sugar, vinegar and salt for
30–45 minutes until vegetables are soft.
Then add the mustard, curry, turmeric and
flour. Simmer for another 10 minutes. If too
thick, add small amount of water.
Bottle in plastic-capped jars, vinegar will
corrode metal lids.

Makes 6 x 500ml jars

Zucchini pickles

Dulcie Martin, Morisset/Lake Macquarie Show

As well as winning the Champion Exhibit at Morisset Show and Newcastle shows, this recipe won the Medallion for Excellence Sydney Royal Show in 2009. It must be good.

Ingredients

1kg (2 lb) zucchini, thinly sliced
1 tablespoon salt
4 small onions, finely sliced
2 teaspoons turmeric
2 teaspoons caraway seeds
2 teaspoons peppercorns
½ teaspoon mustard
4 cups white sugar
4 cups white vinegar

Method

Put the zucchini in bowl, cover with water, add salt and let stand for 2 hours. Add the onions. Drain all liquid off.
Put all other ingredients in saucepan and boil for 1 minute. Pour over zucchini and onions and simmer for 5–10 minutes, then bottle.

Makes 4 x 500ml jars

Photo courtesy Rural Press

Plum rum chutney

Hazel Cameron, Walcha Show

Ingredients

2kg (4½ lb) blood plums, stoned
500g (1 lb) Granny Smith apples, cored
500g (1 lb) raisins
3 cloves garlic, crushed
2 dried chillies
1 tablespoon ground ginger
1 teaspoon ground allspice
375g (13 oz) brown sugar
125ml (4 fl oz) golden syrup
750ml (25 fl oz) cider vinegar
2 tablespoons rum

Method

Combine all the ingredients, except rum, in a saucepan and stir until boiling. Cook uncovered, stirring now and again, for about 1 hour or until thick. Add rum and simmer for a further 5 minutes. Bottle into warm jars. Seal when cold.

. . . .

Apple & date chutney

Vicki Lawrence, Dorrigo Show

Ingredients

2 cups brown vinegar
1 cup brown sugar, firmly packed
1 tablespoon grated fresh ginger
2 small chillies, chopped
1 teaspoon white mustard seeds
2 cups water
3 large apples, peeled and chopped
2 cups dates
2 cups raisins
2 medium onions chopped

Method

Combine vinegar, sugar, ginger, chilli, mustard seeds and water in a large saucepan. Stir over heat until sugar is dissolved. Stir in apples, dates, raisins and onions and bring to boil. Simmer uncovered for about 1 hour, or until mixture is thick. Pour into hot, sterilised jars and seal.

Apricot chutney

Jane Amos, Mungindi Show

Ingredients

1.8kg (4 lb) ripe apricots (can also use peaches)
1.3kg (3 lb) minced onion
950ml (2 pints) white vinegar
450g (1 lb) minced sultanas
1.3kg (3 lb) brown sugar
4 teaspoons salt
2 tablespoons ground ginger
2 teaspoons allspice
1 teaspoon pepper

Method

Place the apricots and onions in a saucepan with the vinegar and boil until just cooked. Put in the remaining ingredients and boil a further half hour. Bottle and seal.

Corn relish

Vikki Fletcher, Grafton Show

As an option, Vikki suggests mixing 200g (7 oz) of this corn relish with 250g (8 oz) cream cheese and a little milk, to help mixing, to make a nice dip.

Ingredients

½ cup malt vinegar
2 cups white vinegar
1 cup sugar (raw or white)
550g (1 lb) whole corn kernels, preserved or tinned, drained
1 medium-sized onion, chopped
½ cup chopped celery
¼ cup chopped green capsicum
¼ cup chopped red capsicum
2½ level tablespoons cornflour
1 level teaspoon dry mustard
1 teaspoon mustard seeds (optional)

Method

In a large saucepan add ½ cup of malt vinegar, 1¾ cups white vinegar and sugar and stir over low heat until sugar is dissolved, then bring to the boil. Add corn, onion, celery and capsicum and simmer for 20 minutes with lid on. Blend cornflour, mustard and the mustard seeds, if desired, with the remaining ¼ cup vinegar and add to the rest of the mixture. Bring back to the boil until the mixture thickens, keep stirring.
Pour into hot sterilised jars.

Makes 4 small jars

Corn relish

Tomato relish

Ros Edwards, Parkes Show

Ros get lots of excess fruit from friends to make into jams, pickles, relishes. She gives them away to church members, parcelled up as gifts, for use in sandwiches, scones at caterings, to charity for the raising of much needed funds and each year several hundred jars are sent to the CWA Tea Rooms at the Sydney Royal Easter Show. This recipe is a family favourite.

Ingredients

500g (1 lb) white onions, chopped
500g (1 lb) ripe tomatoes, finely chopped
1 tablespoon fine salt
1 cup sugar
1 tablespoon curry powder
1 tablespoon mustard powder
2 tablespoons cornflour
1 cup white vinegar

Method

Place onions and tomatoes in a pot, sprinkle with salt, add the sugar, curry powder and mustard powder, bring to boil and simmer for 10 minutes.
Thicken with cornflour mixed with a little vinegar and simmer for a further 5 minutes. Bottle and seal with plastic lids.

Makes 5 x 500ml jars

Tomato relish

Joyce Zeidler, Peak Hill Show

Here is another tomato relish recipe using mustard for a different flavour. Joyce says this recipe comes from 'way back' and has been passed down through the family.

Ingredients

1.8kg (4 lb) ripe tomatoes, peeled and chopped
907g (2 lb) onions, peeled and chopped
8 level teaspoons salt
1 pint of vinegar
3 carrots, grated
907g (2 lb) sugar
scant dessertspoon mustard
scant dessertspoon mild curry powder
dessertspoon tumeric
½ cup plain flour

Method

Place the tomatoes and onions in a bowl, sprinkle with salt and stand overnight. Next day, strain off liquid, add vinegar and carrot. Cook on stove until onion is tender, then add sugar. Mix mustard, curry powder, turmeric and flour to paste with a touch of vinegar and add to tomato mixture to thicken. Boil slowly for a further 20 minutes. Bottle while hot, but don't seal until cold.

. . . .

Rita's tomato relish

Denny Anderson, Crookwell Show

This recipe is from Denny's husband's great grandmother. She says this relish is terrific with cold roasts, salads or freshly buttered hot toast.

Ingredients

2.7kg (6 lb) tomatoes, cut in small pieces
907g (2 lb) onions, chopped finely
½ cup salt
vinegar, to cover
675g (1½ lb) sugar
2 tablespoons curry powder
2 dessertspoons mustard powder
2 tablespoons cornflour
1 teaspoon cloves
1 teaspoon cinnamon
1 teaspoon nutmeg
1 teaspoon ginger

Method

Place the tomatoes and onions in a pot with the salt. Cover and stand overnight. Next day, par off the brine. Put tomatoes and onions in large pan and almost cover with vinegar. Bring to the boil, add sugar and stir well. Mix the curry powder, mustard powder and cornflour together and add to the pot. Stir until thick. Boil for 45 minutes, then add the cloves, cinnamon, nutmeg and ginger. Stir well. Cool and bottle.

Makes 12 x 500ml jars

Preserved fruit in syrup

Norma Cleal, Warialda Show

Ingredients

Select good eating fruit of your choice,
all the same size, not too ripe

Method

Wash the fruit well and dry.
Cut and seed if needed. Wash again.
Prepare bottles by cleaning very well.
Prepare syrup. Pack fruit in bottles.
Pour syrup over fruit until slightly overflowing
and then place lid on top.

Syrup

Ingredients

1 tablespoon sugar
6 cups water

Method

Add sugar and water to saucepan on stove
and bring to boil, stirring slowly. Dissolve
sugar completely, then simmer for 5 minutes.

Tomato sauce

Mia Cambridge, Glen Innes Show

Ingredients

5.4kg (12 lb) tomatoes, chopped
907g (2 lb) onions, chopped
28g (1 oz) garlic, chopped
85g (3 oz) salt
28g (1 oz) cloves
28g (1 oz) ground ginger
cayenne pepper, to taste
568ml (1 pint) vinegar
1kg (2 lb) sugar

Method

Put the tomatoes, onions, garlic, salt, cloves, ginger and pepper into a pot on the stove and boil slowly for two hours. Strain through a colander and add the vinegar and sugar. Boil again until thick. Let cool before bottling and corking.

Plum sauce

Ros Edwards, Parkes Show

Ingredients

3kg (6½ lb) plums
1.5kg (3 lb) sugar
1.75 litres (60 fl oz) vinegar
6 teaspoons salt
1 tablespoon black pepper
1 teaspoon cayenne pepper
¼ cup whole cloves
½ cup ground ginger

Method

Put all ingredients together in a saucepan. Bring to boil, then simmer gently until all stones come away cleanly from the plums. This should take about 1½ hours. Strain through a colander or put through a blender to make smooth. Bottle and seal using plastic-capped jars.

Makes 6–8 x 600ml bottles

. . . .

Worcestershire sauce

Lyn Sjolander, Bellinger Show

Ingredients

3 cups brown vinegar
½ cup treacle
½ cup plum jam
75g (2½ oz) onion, chopped
1 clove garlic, crushed
¼ teaspoon chilli powder
1 teaspoon ground allspice
¼ teaspoon ground cloves
¼ teaspoon cayenne pepper

Method

Combine all ingredients in a large saucepan.
Stir over heat until mixture boils and simmer,
uncovered, for 1 hour, stirring occasionally.
Strain mixture into hot, sterilised jars.
Seal when cold.

Mayonnaise

Debbie Allan, Griffith Show

This is a simple and traditional recipe from Debbie's grandmother from Rottnest Island in 1939.

Ingredients

3 tablespoons milk
3 tablespoons white sugar
3 tablespoons brown vinegar
2 eggs
1 tablespoon butter
1 teaspoon mustard

Method

Place all ingredients into a bowl. Stir over a pan of hot water until thick and bottle. Keeps for weeks. Especially good in potato salad.

Jams, jellies, marmalades & spreads

. . . .

Apricot jam

Jo Roughley, Walgett Show

Ingredients

1.5kg (3 lb) apricots, just-ripe,
peeled and sliced
1.25kg (2¾ lb) sugar
juice of 1 lemon

Method

Put the apricots in a saucepan and sprinkle over 2 tablespoons of the sugar. Let stand overnight or until syrup forms. Cook gently on the stove until apricots are tender. Add remaining sugar and lemon juice. Boil rapidly until it gels. Bottle and seal.

Tip

To test if your jam is ready, when it begins to fall from the spoon in thick sheets, spoon a small quantity of the jam onto a cold saucer and place in the freezer for 1 minute. Remove from the freezer and run your finger over the jam. If it wrinkles, to touch—meaning a skin has formed— the jam has 'gelled' and is ready for bottling.

. . . .

Berry jam

Leonie Lee, Glen Innes Show

Ingredients

2kg (4½ lb) berries such as raspberries,
youngberries, boysenberries etc.
2kg (4½ lb) sugar, warmed

Method

Place berries in a large saucepan and
simmer, covered, on the stove until soft.
Add the warmed sugar and stir to dissolve.
Boil gently until the jam sets when tested.
Spoon into sterilised bottles.

Blackberry jam

Blackberry jam

Denny Anderson, Crookwell Show

Denny says this recipe is best using fresh-picked blackberries from good bushes. Delicious with hot scones and fresh cream!

Ingredients

1kg (2 lb) blackberries
75ml (2½ fl oz) lemon juice
1kg (2 lb) sugar
50g Jamsetta
(available from supermarkets)

Method

Preheat oven to 230°C (450°F).
Remove leaves and stalks from the blackberries, rinse and drain. Put into a heavy bottom saucepan, squeeze lemon juice over and cook on low heat until berries are soft, about 15–20 minutes.
Meanwhile heat sugar in microwave for 3 minutes. Remove and add Jamsetta. Stir until combined. Add to cooked berries and stir slowly bringing back to the boil.
Boil for 4–5 minutes.
Test by placing a spoonful of jam on a cold saucer to see if a skin forms on the top.
When a skin forms, the jam is ready.
When jam has formed a skin, take off heat and leave to sit for 15 minutes. Place jars on heatproof tray and spoon jam into jars right to the top and seal. Leave to cool.
Let sit for 2–3 days before eating.

Makes 6 small jars

. . . .

Boysenberry & plum jam

Ida Whiteman, Camden Show

This is an easy recipe. You can make as much or as little as you need by cooking by proportion.

Ingredients

1kg (2 lb) boysenberries
1kg (2 lb) plums
2kg (4½ lb) sugar
lemon juice, to taste

Method

Clean and hull boysenberries. Put in a saucepan with a little water on the stove and stir until tender. Wash plums. Put in another saucepan with a little water on the stove and stir until tender. Put through colander to remove stones and skins.

Mix the boysenberries and plums together. Put fruit back in a saucepan and bring to the boil. Take off the heat for a minute while you add the sugar. Stir until sugar dissolved, then boil until it gels. Add lemon juice if desired. Spoon into bottles and seal.

· ·

Dark grape jam

Robyn Schmierer, Singleton Show

Robyn makes this jam from Isabella grapes from a 70-plus-year-old vine growing in her yard in the Hunter Valley.

Ingredients

1.5kg (3 lb) grapes
1kg (2 lb) sugar
juice of 1 lemon

Method

Squeeze pulp out of grapes and boil in a saucepan on stove for 20 minutes.
Strain seeds, add remainng pulp to skins and boil for a further 15–20 minutes.
Add sugar and lemon juice and stir until the sugar dissolves. Bring to boil until setting point is reached. Pour into warm sterilised jars and seal.

· ·

Fig & ginger jam

Diana Lisle, Walcha Show

This jam is a real winner. It gained a perfect score, 100/100, at the 2009 district exhibit competition and had been placed 1st for 3 consecutive years in the preserves section of the RAS arts and craft competition.

Ingredients

1kg (2 lb) fresh figs
800g (1½ lb) white sugar, warmed
1½ teaspoons citric acid
1 tablespoon brown sugar
1 tablespoon finely chopped glazed ginger

Method

Preheat oven to 120°C (250°F). Wash and rinse bottles and place in oven to sterilise while cooking the jam.

Wash and dry figs and remove the thick part of the stalk. Chop the figs evenly into small pieces and place in a large microwave dish. Cover and microwave until the fruit is soft and cooked. Transfer cooked fruit to a stainless-steel preserving pan, add the citric acid and brown sugar and mix well.

Place the pan on the stove and bring to a simmer. Add the warmed sugar and dissolve. Increase the heat to a rapid boil. Remove any impurities from the side of the pan during this process by skimming across the surface with a spoon. Test for setting by placing a teaspoonful of jam on a cold saucer, and place in the fridge for 3 minutes. If the jam sets, it is ready. Just before you remove the pan from the heat, add the glazed ginger and stir well. Set aside to cool for 8–10 minutes, bottle and seal.

. . . .

Fig jam

Margaret Bradley, Trundle Show

Ingredients

1kg (2 lb) figs
750g (1½ lb) of sugar

Method

Place figs in a saucepan, cover with water and simmer until tender. Mash and add sugar. Stir until sugar is well dissolved. Boil until mixture begins to thicken or gels, stirring occasionally to stop sticking to the bottom of pan. Put into sterilised hot jars and seal.

· ·

Melon, orange & lemon jam

Mia Cambridge, Glenn Innes Show

Ingredients

6.8kg (15 lb) melon, cut into small pieces
6 lemons, chopped
6 oranges, chopped
sugar

Method

Put a jam melon in a large saucepan, cover with cold water and let stand overnight.
In a separate saucepan put the lemon and orange pieces and cover with boiling water (about 6 cups) and let soak overnight.
The next day, combine the fruit into one saucepan, including liquid and boil until soft, about 1–1½ hours.
Strain in muslin cloth, overnight and save the liquid. Return the liquid to the pot and add sugar—allow 1 cup of sugar to 1 cup of liquid—Boil for 1½–2 hours or until it gels when tested. Bottle and seal.

Makes 10 x 500ml jars

· ·

Peach jam

Ann Elder, Bungendore Show

Ann only started making jams seven years ago but she has exhibited successfully in the Bungendore Show and other local shows ever since. In 2005, 2008 and 2009 she was awarded 'Most Outstanding' for her jams. Here are some of her favourites.

Ingredients

1kg (2 lb) peaches, peeled, stoned and quartered
1 cup water
2 tablespoons lemon juice
750g (1½ lb) sugar

Method

Put peaches in saucepan and cover with water. Cook on high until peaches are soft. Add lemon juice and sugar. Return to heat and stir until sugar is dissolved.
Bring to boil and boil briskly until setting point is reached. Cool slightly and pack and seal in sterilised jars.

Makes about 500ml

Plum & port jam

Ann Elder Bungendore Show

Ingredients

500g (1 lb) plums, washed, stoned and cut in half
½ cup water
1½ cups sugar
2 tablespoons port

Method

Place plums and water in a large saucepan. Boil until plums are pulpy and soft. Add sugar and stir until dissolved. Return to the boil and boil briskly until setting point is reached. Remove from heat and stir in the port. Cool for a few minutes then pack and seal in sterilised jars.

Makes about 500ml

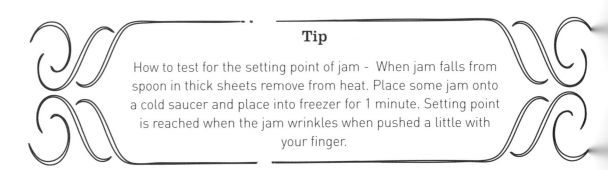

Tip

How to test for the setting point of jam - When jam falls from spoon in thick sheets remove from heat. Place some jam onto a cold saucer and place into freezer for 1 minute. Setting point is reached when the jam wrinkles when pushed a little with your finger.

Dark plum jam

Anthea and Marg Parsons, Nowra Show

Ingredients

2kg (4½ lb) blood plums, (I recommend Teagan Blue plums) cut in half and stones removed
1.5kg (3 lb) sugar, warmed
½ cup lemon juice

Method

Place plums in a large saucepan with 2 cups water and bring slowly to the boil. Reduce heat and simmer, covered, for about 40 minutes until the fruit is soft.
Add the warmed sugar and lemon juice and stir with a wooden spoon until the sugar is dissolved. Bring to the boil again and boil for 20–25 minutes, removing any scum from the surface with a slotted spoon.
Start testing for setting. When jam falls from spoon in thick sheets remove from heat
Place some jam onto a cold saucer and place into freezer for 1 minute. Setting point is reached when the jam will wrinkle when pushed a little with your finger.
Pour immediately into clean warm jars and seal.

Tip

How to test for the setting point of jam - When jam falls from spoon in thick sheets remove from heat. Place some jam onto a cold saucer and place into freezer for 1 minute. Setting point is reached when the jam wrinkles when pushed a little with your finger.

The Country Show Cookbook

Photo courtesy Rural Press

. . . .

Quince jam

Ida Whiteman, Camden Show

Ingredients

quinces
white sugar
lemon juice (optional)

Method

Clean well and put in saucepan as many quinces as it will hold. Cover with water and boil until quite tender. Remove from saucepan, quarter and put cores (and skins if you wished) back in saucepan of water and boil for half and hour. Strain through a colander and reserve juice. Slice quince pulp into small pieces, add to juice and measure in cupfuls. Allowing 1 cup of quinces to 1 cup of white sugar, add sugar to the quinces. Return to stove and stir well until all the sugar is dissolved before the mixture boils. Boil all together until it gels and colour pleases. Lemon juice may be added 5 minutes before taking off stove if necessary.

Raspberry jam

Beryl Schaefer OAM, Cobargo Show

Beryl started exhibiting jams and jellies in the early 60s and this soon brought her to the attention of a Mrs Mills, a judge from Goulburn. She was soon preparing jams and jellies for the Southern District Display at the Royal Easter Show.

Ingredients

0.5kg (1 lb) raspberries
0.5kg (1 lb) sugar, warmed
a little water

Method

Place fruit and a little water in a preserving pan and bring to boil. Stir from time to time with a wooden spoon so it does not stick. Add warmed sugar and stir ocassionally, skimming any impurities that rise to the surface thoroughly.
No hard and fast rule can be used for time before it is ready, as it depends on the fruit. When a little jam is poured on a saucer and it sets in a few minutes, it is ready.
Bottle in sterilised jars.

Tip

To warm sugar, Genaveve Press from Robertson suggests heating it for 1 minute on high in the microwave. Margaret Mears from Bulahdelah warms her sugar by spreading it on a tray in a warm oven for a few minutes.

. . . .

Raspberry jam

Genaveve Press, Robertson Show

Genaveve is 14 years old and won Junior Champion Preserve at Robertson for this recipe. It has been handed down from her grandmother. It was her great great grandmother's recipe.

Ingredients

2kg (4½ lb) fresh or frozen raspberries
2kg (4½ lb) white sugar
juice of 2 very large or 3 small lemons

Method

Boil fruit until it pulps down—this will take about 10 minutes on simmer—stirring occasionally. Warm sugar for 1 minute on high in microwave. Add to the pulp with the lemon juice and stir in until dissolved.
Bring to boil and cook on rolling boil for about 10 minutes or until temperature comes up to 221°C (425°F) on a thermometer.
Remove from the heat and stir occasionally for 3–5 minutes, before bottling and sealing tightly.

Makes about 6 x medium-sized jars

Strawberry & rhubarb jam

Ann Elder, Bungendore Show

Ingredients

250g (8 oz) firm strawberries, hulled,
washed and halved
250g (8 oz) rhubarb, trimmed, washed
and cut into small pieces
2¼ cups sugar

Method

Put all of the fruit into a non-metallic bowl
and cover with 1½ cups of the sugar.
Leave to stand overnight.
The next day, transfer the fruit to a large
saucepan and add the remaining ¾ cup sugar.
Bring to boil slowly and boil briskly, stir
occasionally until setting point is reached.
Cool slightly and pack and seal in
sterilised jars.

Makes about 1 litre of jam

. . . .

Strawberry jam

Margaret Bradley, Trundle Show

Ingredients

1 kg (2 lb) strawberries
juice of 1 lemon
¾ cup sugar

Method

Place strawberries and lemon juice in a large saucepan and cook fruit well, until it is soft.
Mash and add sugar.
Stir well and boil until it gels. Stir now and then to stop sticking to the bottom of pan.
Put into sterilised hot jars and seal.

. . . .

Tomato jam

Patricia Williams, Baradine Show

Ingredients

2kg (4½ lb) tomatoes, peeled and cut into pieces
1.5kg (3 lb) sugar
3 lemons, juiced and rind grated

Method

In a heavy based saucepan, place the peeled tomatoes, sugar, lemon rind and lemon juice. Stir over heat until sugar dissolves. Bring to the boil. Boil until jam sets when tested. Pour into heated jars and seal.

. . . .

Tomato & passionfruit jam

Margaret Minnis, Barellan Show

Margaret uses a jam pan to make this recipe. Also called a preserving pan, jam pans are large and wide-brimmed to allow the excess water in the fruit (or vegetables) to evaporate as quickly as possible.

Ingredients

1kg (2 lb) tomatoes, peeled
¾ cup passionfruit
1.25kg (2¾ lb) sugar

Method

Add all ingredients to a jam pan or large saucepan and cook for 30 minutes or until fruit is desired consistency. To gel test every 10 minutes. Pour into sterilised, warm jars. Seal and cool.

Tip

Some fruit is better than others for jams because of the level of pectin in the fruit. When experimenting with new fruit, it's a good idea to test for pectin to see if it's suitable for jam as follows:

Measure 1 tablespoon of rubbing alcohol into a small glass. Add 1 teaspoon of extracted fruit juice and let stand 2 minutes. If a good solid mass forms, enough pectin is naturally present in the fruit juice to make jam. If only a small, weak mass forms, there is not enough pectin to form a gel and a commercial pectin or a fruit high in pectin should be combined with it. Don't taste this mixture!

· ·

Apple jelly

Jenny Baker, Cobargo Show

This apple jelly is tasty with chesse and bread, or try it on pikelets.

Ingredients

2kg (4½ lb) apples, roughly chopped,
do not peel or core
1 litre (32 fl oz) water (approximately)
juice of 1 lemon
sugar

Method

Put apples, water and lemon juice in a
saucepan—they should be just covered with
water. Simmer gently, covered, until apples
are soft and pulpy—about 30 minutes.
Uncover and cook a little more briskly until
liquid is reduced by about a third.
Strain through a jelly bag (piece of calico) into
a bowl. Leave overnight. Do not squeeze bag.
Measure the liquid and allow ½ kg (1 lb)
sugar to every ½ litre (pint) of liquid.
Put into a saucepan and stir over low heat
until sugar dissolves. Bring to boil and boil
fairly briskly until setting point is reached.
Remove pan from heat. Skim any scum, then
bottle and seal.

Jams, jellies, marmalades & spreads

. . . .

Fruit jelly

Leonie Lee, Glen Innes Show

Ingredients

Slightly under-ripe fruit such as apples,
berries, quinces, plums, apricots or lemons,
chopped
sugar, warmed

Method

Place fruit into a large saucepan and cover with water. Boil gently, covered, until fruit is soft. Strain through a jelly cloth—do not squeeze. Measure the liquid and allow 1 cup of sugar for each cup of liquid. Heat liquid, add warmed sugar and stir to dissolve. Boil quickly until the jelly sets when tested. Bottle and label.

Note: a pectin test should be done on fruits not previously used for jelly.

· ·

Crabapple jelly

Kay Farlow, Glen Innes Show

Ingredients

Crabapples, just ripe
sugar

Method

Wash and wipe the crabapples, cutting away any defects. Slice and place in a pan, just covered with water. Boil gently until soft, 30–35 minutes. Strain through a calico bag. Measure, cup-to-cup, an equal quantity of sugar. Add the sugar and liquid to the pan and boil rapidly until it responds to test on cold saucer. Place in hot, clean jars and seal.

. . . .

Guava jelly

Corrie Hayes, Grafton Show

Ingredients

guavas
sugar
1 dessertspoon lemon juice

Method

Wash and slice the desired quantity of fruit into quarters and place them in a preserving pan—more fruit produces more juice and thus more jelly. This recipe is dependent on amount of juice obtained after straining. Add enough water to cover the fruit then crush with a wooden spoon. Boil slowly until soft. Strain through a cheesecloth, folded over at least twice, so only the juice of the fruit flows through. Measure amount of juice by cup. Return juice to preserving pan and bring to boil. Boil quickly for 5 minutes then add 1 cup of heated sugar to each cup of juice and lemon juice. Stir with wooden spoon until sugar is dissolved. Boil rapidly until mixture jellies, when tested.
Pour carefully into preheated jars. When cold, place lids on and seal.

Quince jelly

Daphne Williams, Condoblin Show

Ingredients

3–4 quinces
water
juice of 1 lemon juice
sugar

Method

Wash quinces and roughly cut up without peeling or removing cores. Place in a large saucepan and add cold water to just cover. Bring to the boil and simmer until quinces are soft and pink. Strain through a muslin cloth overnight, do not rub or squeeze. Measure liquids in a jug allowing 600g (21 oz) of sugar per 500ml (16 fl oz) of liquid. Place liquid and lemon juice into a saucepan and bring to the boil. Then add the sugar and stir until sugar has dissolved. Boil rapidly for around 30 minutes, but do not stir as this will cause the syrup to go cloudy.
Place a teaspoon of jelly on a cold saucer to test if it gels. Boil longer and repeat if necessary. Once syrup gels, place in warm bottles and seal.
Cooking times may vary depending on the ripeness of the fruit.

....

Basic marmalade

Ros Edwards, Parkes Show

Ingredients

1kg (2 lb) fruit, any citrus fruit or a combination of citrus fruits, e.g. oranges, mandarins, grapefruit, lemons, lemonades, limes, cumquats, tangelloes
pinch of salt
2 litres water
2kg (4½ lb) sugar, warmed
juice of 1½ lemons

Method

Cut fruit to preferred size and soak overnight. White pith should be removed from grapefruit and thick-skinned lemons.
Put fruit in a boiler with salt. Bring to boil and simmer, with the lid on, for about 1½ hours.
Add the sugar and lemon juice and boil rapidly. Jam is ready when fine frothy bubbles appear—about an hour.
Bottle in clean jars and seal while hot.
Note: For variety, ginger or passionfruit or carrots can be added to change flavour of single fruits.

Makes 6–7 x 500ml jars

. . . .

Sweet orange marmalade

Dulcie Wibrecury OAM, Comboyne Show

Ingredients

4 large, thin-skinned oranges
12 cups water
9 cups sugar, warmed

Method

Wash the oranges, cut into very thin slices and remove seeds. Soak seeds in a cup of water. Place sliced fruit in a bowl, cover with water and stand overnight. Next morning, add strained juice from seeds and sugar, stirring with a wooden spoon until dissolved. Boil quickly until it jellies when tested. Allow to cool a little. Then pour carefully into warm jars. When cold cover down airtight.

· ·

Orange marmalade

Margaret Mears, Bulahdelah Show

Ingredients

4 good-looking oranges
1 large lemon
6 cups water
0.5kg (1 lb) sugar, warmed

Method

Peel thinly the rind from 2 oranges. Cut rind into fine strips or put into a blender and blend gently. Put the rind into a small saucepan, cover with water and cook for 45 minutes. Put aside. Roughly chop up all fruit and put into large pot. Cover with water and cook for 1 hour. Strain, keeping the juice and discarding the orange bits. Measure the juice and put back into the pot. Add the juice and rind and bring to the boil.

For every cup of juice place one cup of sugar on a tray and warm in the oven to heat through. Add the sugar to the liquid and continue to cook until thickened—don't let it boil over. Remove from heat. Test the jam on a cold plate, it will form wrinkles when ready.
Pour into warm jars and seal.

Lemon butter

Orange marmalade

· ·

Apricot conserve

Beris Jones, Ganmain Show

Ingredients

2kg (4½ lb) apricots, halved and stones
removed
2kg (4½ lb) sugar
2 cups water
2 tablespoons lemon juice

Method

Place apricots, water and half the sugar (1kg)
in saucepan, bring to the boil and simmer
gently for 5 minutes. Add remaining sugar
and lemon juice and continue to boil until
setting point is reached.
Put into warm, dry jars. Seal and cover.
Store in a cool, dry place.

Quince honey

May Hill, Berrigan Show

May Hill has been showing at Berrigan Show for over 70 years and also is one of the many stewards in the Cooking/Art/Craft pavilion, who have been the backbone of the pavilion for over 40 years.

Ingredients

9 cups water
6 cups sugar
3 large quinces, grated

Method

In a large pot boil water and sugar. Add the grated quince and continue to boil until it gels and quinces turn pink.

....

Lemon cheese

Dianne Kelly, Walgett Show

Dianne won the Jar of Lemon Cheese Class for Jams and Cookery in the Cookery Section, and also Champion Exhibit, Jams and Preserves at 2008 Walgett Show with this recipe.

Ingredients

6 eggs
450g (1 lb) sugar
juice of 6 lemons
rind of 2 lemons
113g (¼ lb) butter

Method

Beat eggs with butter and sugar. Add lemon juice and lemon rind. Put in double saucepan and stir. Allow only to come to boiling point and remove from stove. Bottle and seal well.

. . . .

Passionfruit butter

Marg Parsons and Anthea Parsons, Nowra Show

Ingredients

8 eggs
1½ cups castor sugar
3 teaspoons lemon rind, grated
⅓ cup lemon juice
400g (13 oz) soft unsalted butter, soft
1 cup passionfruit pulp

Method

Beat eggs and strain into a heatproof bowl. Stir in castor sugar, lemon rind, lemon juice and butter. Strain passionfruit pulp and discard half the seeds. Place in bowl altogether over a pan of simmering water. Stir until the butter has melted and all the sugar has dissolved. Keep stirring constantly for 20–25 minutes until the mixture thickly coats the back of a wooden spoon.
Pour into clean warm jars and seal while hot. Refrigerate when cold. This jam will keep in the refrigerator up to two months.

Makes about 4 x 250ml jars

Lemon butter

Kate Cunningham, Condoblin Show

Ingredients

125g (4 oz) butter
2 cups sugar
½ tablespoon finely grated lemon zest
juice of 3 medium-sized lemons
4 large eggs, well beaten

Method

In a saucepan combine butter, sugar, zest and juice and stir until completely dissolved and shiny. Take off heat and leave until warm. Add eggs and return to low to medium heat, stirring continuously until the mixture is thick. Pour into sterilised jars while hot.

Variations

Lime—replace lemon juice and zest with lime juice and zest

Orange—125g (4 oz) butter, 1¹/₃–1½ cups sugar, 4 eggs, juice of 1 large orange and 1 tablespoon zest

Passionfruit—same as for Orange Butter (above) and add passionfruit pulp (but a few seeds only), plus juice of half a lemon.

See picture on page 249.

Recipe Index